CRYSTAL ZODIAC FOR BEGINNERS

CRYSTAL ZODIAC

FOR BEGINNERS

A Practical Guide to Harnessing the Power of Astrology and Crystals

APRIL PFENDER

ROCKRIDGE
PRESS

For general information on our other products and services or to obtain technical support, please contact our Customer Care Department within the United States at (866) 744-2665, or outside the United States at (510) 253-0500.

Rockridge Press publishes its books in a variety of electronic and print formats. Some content that appears in print may not be available in electronic books, and vice versa.

Interior and Cover Designer: Scott Wooledge
Art Producer: Alyssa Williams
Editor: Brian Sweeting
Production Editor: Ellina Litmanovich
Production Manager: Jose Olivera

Copyright Page: Illustrations © Blixa 6 Studios/Creative Market; Photos used under license from Shutterstock.com, Alamy

Paperback ISBN: 978-1-63878-439-5
eBook ISBN: 978-1-63878-695-5
R0

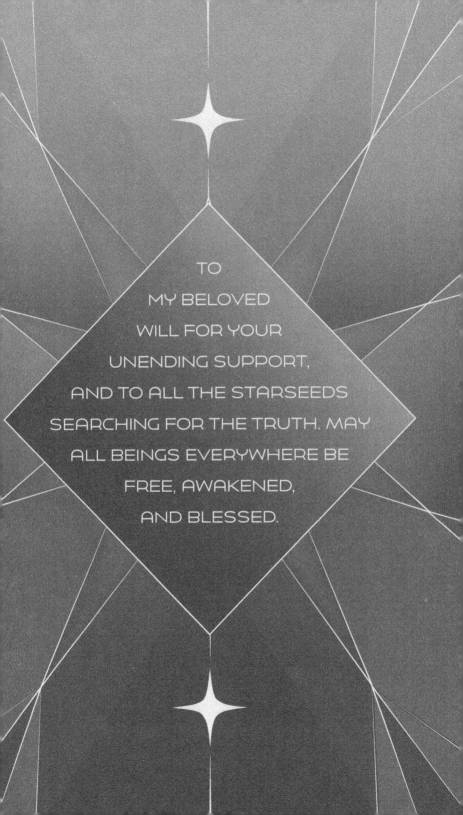

TO

MY BELOVED

WILL FOR YOUR

UNENDING SUPPORT,

AND TO ALL THE STARSEEDS

SEARCHING FOR THE TRUTH. MAY

ALL BEINGS EVERYWHERE BE

FREE, AWAKENED,

AND BLESSED.

CONTENTS

INTRODUCTION. viii
HOW TO USE THIS BOOK xi

PART I: . An Introduction to Astrology & Crystals . . . 1
CHAPTER 1: Astrology 101 2
CHAPTER 2: Crystals 101 .21

PART II: . Deepen Your Knowledge
of the Signs & Crystals 35
CHAPTER 3: Zodiac Profiles 36
CHAPTER 4: Crystal Profiles 47

PART III: Crystal Practices for
Sun, Moon & Rising Signs 85
CHAPTER 5: Crystal Practices for Sun Signs. 86
CHAPTER 6: Crystal Practices for Moon Signs 99
CHAPTER 7: Crystal Practices for Rising Signs 112
CHAPTER 8: Q & A 125

A FINAL WORD. 130
GLOSSARY. 132
RESOURCES 134
REFERENCES. 136
INDEX 137

INTRODUCTION

Astrology and crystals have captured the minds and hearts of people everywhere for millennia. Spanning across eons, the stars above and the crystals on Earth have long been points of fascination and intrigue. You don't need to be a mystic to appreciate these natural wonders rich in history and allure. They are here to tell a story and to remind us of who we are, where we came from, and where we are going.

I'm guessing our first experiences with this natural world felt similar. I was spellbound when I first saw crystals at a young age. My personal favorite, the amethyst, naturally calmed me, and its lovely energy drew me right in. That's because we tend to sense and feel energy with our intuitive self before we consciously recognize its form and function. My lifelong love for rocks grew as I became increasingly mesmerized by the gemstones I encountered. Over the years, they became useful tools for my Reiki healing practice, and I saw them helping my clients in both subtle and overt ways, increasing their well-being and quality of life. Crystals have the power to calm, energize, increase focus, de-stress your life, and clear your energy. For me, crystals were a gatekeeper to a deeper world of transcendence, and meditation was my vehicle. They enhanced my personal practice over the decades, and I've led thousands of students to find their own connection to crystals through guided meditations to help them discover the keys to their own healing.

It wasn't until later in life that I got curious about astrology, and another layer became awakened within me on my spiritual path. I was skeptical and doubted that a story about the stars could make much sense for my life. Yet every time I looked up a transit or specific sign and started to draw my own associations, everything fit like a missing puzzle piece in the mystery that is life. Astrology offers a glimpse into our soul's cycles and behaviors and helps us gain important insights to guide ourselves through change. Astrology is meant to stimulate self-reflection, which can transform your life. You don't need to have a religion or be "spiritual" to plug into the inherent gifts of illumination it provides.

As a Reiki master teacher, meditation instructor, and quantum healer, I have learned many ways to enhance the mind/body connection. Even when we aren't actively working on healing, we should always strive to be the best possible version of ourselves. The tools presented in this book are useful to anyone discovering journeying along the path of mindfulness, intention, and personal growth. Astrology and crystals enhance one another, and the practices presented here are designed to complement your natural strengths.

This book is written for those who are new to astrology and crystals and wish to gain knowledge about their basic functions. If you are a more advanced practitioner, you can use this book as a brushup, an easy reference guide, or a teaching tool. I encourage you to go through the exercises and share this book with others who may be just starting on their path of self-discovery. You never know where someone is on their path, and this could be the information needed to awaken their inner gifts.

We will review foundational information to cover all the basics you'll need to sufficiently approach astrology and crystals first, and then we'll explore profiles of key elements such as the Sun, Moon, and rising signs, along with specific crystals' qualities. This book will help you apply this knowledge using step-by-step practices. Imagine yourself aligning with the flow of the universe as things start to make more sense and you glide through transformation periods with more ease.

I wish you many blessings on your journey, and I'm optimistic that you'll have a lot of fun along the way. I hope this book ignites a spark of joy within that wasn't there before and begins to open new pathways to your great awakening. After all, when we directly experience the magic of the stars and the earth, we can more deeply piece together the most important question of them all: "Why am I here and what is my purpose?" May this book bless you with much enjoyment as you discover this for yourself. You are exactly where you are meant to be!

HOW TO USE THIS BOOK

The practices in this book are short in length and powerful in impact. As with any new practice, incorporating these modalities will take your attention and time. Learning is a process, so go easy on yourself if you aren't picking things up right away. Illumination will come from consistent practice and integration. There's not a one-size-fits-all wellness practice, so simply take what resonates and leave the rest, while you nourish your mind, body, and spirit. As simple as it sounds, mindfulness and attention take energy, so patience is key. Juggling work, relationships, and the rest of your personal life takes up plenty of time, so be intentional in setting aside time for spiritual practices, introspection, and self-care. As your knowledge builds, you'll find a rhythm that's right for you, and you'll be able to revisit your favorite exercises or try new ones that are particularly helpful for your zodiac placements.

In the first part of the book, we'll cover the basics of astrology, then crystals separately. We'll talk about what these are, how they came to be, and how they can enhance your life. There's much to know, and once you are comfortable with this book, I encourage you to practice weaving your new knowledge with different people in your life to discover new aspects of the signs outside your own.

This book is structured for you to take at your own pace while you use astrology and crystals in tandem for a personalized approach to wellness. You can think about astrology as a blueprint to your life, and crystals as the construction material. Neither represent the finished masterpiece, but they work together to assist you in building your best life. Thoughts and actions will come into alignment as you gain valuable insight to behavioral patterns, and you'll start to become deliberate in your actions. This is a path to personal clarity.

PART I

AN INTRODUCTION TO ASTROLOGY & CRYSTALS

There's a lot to learn about astrology and crystals individually. As this book is about using the two together, there are a lot of basics to cover. First, we'll dive into the fundamentals of astrology, including what exactly astrology is, how to use it, and how it can enhance our lives; and then we'll cover essential knowledge about crystals. By part 2 of this book, you'll be ready to combine your knowledge of each to accelerate your path to growth.

CHAPTER 1

ASTROLOGY 101

Although there is no one system that can completely define who you are, astrology aims to unearth the traits and attributes of your personality so you can develop a relationship with the deepest parts of yourself. In this chapter, we'll cover the basics of what exactly astrology is and its origins. This will give you a working definition of the modality and how best to use it. Astrology has a rich history with many branches that have evolved over time to the Western (tropical) system we use today.

Though it's fascinating to track all of the different ways we can interpret the zodiac, focusing on the pieces presented in this book will help you understand how to use it for yourself and those around you. You will learn about the zodiac, your Sun, Moon, and rising signs, the planets, and the twelve houses. You'll also learn how to recognize distinctions between signs by examining qualities like elements and modalities. Let's get started!

WHAT IS ASTROLOGY?

The sky is grouped into constellations, or celestial bodies that tell ancient cosmic stories. It is divided into 360 degrees, with twelve zodiac signs (each taking up thirty degrees). If you took a snapshot of the sky the moment you were born, it would show how all the planets and constellations were positioned and aligned, to the exact degree, as you made your appearance on the earth. Astrology deals with how these placements affect your behaviors, traits, tendencies, weaknesses and strengths. The details of these planetary and zodiac placements, based on the exact date, time, and location in which you were born, make up your natal chart (which we'll discuss later in this chapter), which can be extraordinarily beneficial in helping you understand yourself.

Astrology is not a system of absolutes. When used correctly, it poses questions, rather than telling us about who we are. It holds a mirror in front of you and asks you to go inside, acting like a guidance system that allows you to draw meaning from the correlations between your habits and traits so you can hone your intuition and enhance your innate gifts. Astrology doesn't tell us who we are, but it does allow us to examine our tendencies and the ways in which we interact with the world.

THE STORY OF ASTROLOGY

While the origins of astrology are difficult to trace, there is evidence going back far into history, spanning ancient cultures. Evidence shows that the roots of astrology as we know it today may date back three thousand years, with the communal calendar's development across Babylon, Greece, Rome, China, India, and Mesoamerica. Until the seventeenth century, astrology was a considered a scholarly tradition and dovetailed with astronomy. Eventually, the paths of the disciplines diverged, and astronomy continued under more scientific pursuits, while astrology began to branch out into the mystical realms. The three main types of astrology used today are Western (tropical), Vedic, and Chinese. The tropical system to which we refer in this book is based on the Sun's relationship to the Earth and how close it is to our tropics (the Tropic of Cancer and Tropic of Capricorn).

Today's Western astrology is most commonly known from short newspaper-style horoscopes, but it has much more to offer than those short paragraphs indicate. Astrology is an ancient technology, harnessing the energy of the cosmic cycles to connect us to our origins. Through it, we can gain a greater self-awareness and unlock more of our own spiritual consciousness.

ASTROLOGY CAN ENHANCE YOUR LIFE

Although it's no Magic 8-Ball, the predictive nature of astrology delivers potent insights, lessons, and opportunities to shift your perspective, especially regarding your behaviors and actions. The entire world is in a beautiful awakening state right now—a golden age of consciousness—allowing you to access higher awareness. Knowing how to operate in this world by playing to your own strengths will keep you in a more aligned vibrational state of well-being, more consistently.

Modern astrology is a valuable tool to understand yourself on a deeper level. Recognizing your own temperament and tendencies can help explain why you act the way you do and how you can work with your own energy to break free from toxic cycles while playing to your best qualities. Astrology can shed light on what situations and events are going to have the highest and most beneficial impact on your daily life. The planets, stars, and asteroids move through the sky in their orbits; in astrology, these paths are known as **transits**. Knowing which transits

EXPLORING YOUR NATAL CHART

Part of what makes astrology so fascinating is the fact that you can go so deep, exploring the different layers about yourself that you always knew yet may not have had the words to describe. It's tailored to you and based on the exact moment you chose to come into the world. To get exact information on your astrological elements via your natal chart, it's helpful to know your birth details. You'll want to know details such as the date, exact time, and location of birth. If you are unsure of the time of your birth or aren't able to access that information, you can make an estimate or use 12 p.m. on the day you were born. This will provide you with the majority of your planetary placements. You can use the information to pull a free natal chart reading from one of the many astrology sites that exist.

are occurring can inform your goals and upcoming activities. If you start to pay attention to how you are feeling during certain times (for example, during full or new Moons in a certain Moon cycle), you can plan around the celestial calendar to ensure your success and ease.

Another popular way astrology is used today is to explore compatibility in relationships. It can help you understand how you relate to others on deeper levels to determine how you might get along with someone. By simply noticing where the strengths and weaknesses of each partner lay, you can better manage expectations and navigate situations that may come up over the course of the interactions with your partner. Just remember not to let a horoscope dictate the outcome of a relationship. With a focus on love and compassion, and with the right mindset and intention, any obstacles can be overcome.

NAVIGATING YOUR SUN, MOON & RISING SIGNS

The most common question in astrology is, of course, "What's your sign?" This refers to your Sun sign, which represents your core qualities. Although it's an important question to ask, you are so much more than your Sun sign. Your Moon (lunar) sign, and rising (**ascendant**) sign represent major parts of your psyche, and should always be included in this formula when the information is available. Have you ever noticed that two of your friends who have the same astrological sign are nothing alike? This is why we look at these **"big three"** first. They are the main astrological points that deliver the most significant information in your chart. Determining where these signs fall within your **birth chart** gives you access to a more complete picture of who you are.

Sun Sign

Your Sun sign is the zodiac placement that the Sun was in at the time of your birth. It represents the most relevant information you can access in regards to your personality and how you show up and play in the world. This is an essential aspect to your sense of self, and remains relatively unchanged through your life. Your Sun sign informs your disposition, ego, personality, vital energies, and purpose. It represents what you want in life, your identity, and your truest nature.

Moon Sign

Your lunar, or Moon sign, is the zodiac placement that the Moon was in at the time of your birth. If you think about the way the Sun and Moon relate to one another in the sky, you can connect how this relationship also plays out in your chart. The Moon is the luminary representing your private inner self, intuition, and emotional foundation. The Moon influences the way you respond to the world around you, how you process your feelings, and how you nurture yourself and others.

Rising Sign

Your rising sign, or ascendant, is the zodiac placement that was rising on the eastern horizon at the time of your birth. This placement is the way others perceive you, or the image you project into the world. Because it is an outward-facing aspect, people will interact with this facet of your personality often, like your Sun sign, and their combined effects create the picture others have of you. Think of this one like a mask you wear on the outside. This placement determines all the placements of the houses, or areas of life, and where they are in your chart, so it is included in your big three.

THE 12 ZODIAC SIGNS

In Western astrology, the zodiac is divided into twelve signs, which correspond to the constellations. These star groups are marked out by the path the Sun travels during the course of a year. Each sign has its own energies, qualities, and attributes that influence and guide your life and the way you are. Your signs are like a costume that you wear, or the style in which you respond to and interact with the world.

Certain zodiac signs play well together, and some have a tendency to oppose each other. Compatibility should be based on a full picture, including the **elements,** planetary **aspects** (when two or more planets line up in the sky at certain angles), and houses into which the signs fall in your birth chart. In addition, each sign holds two sides: its evolved state and its shadow side (its merits or detriments). Each sign brings a unique and individual outlook to life. Much of the way we interact can be attributed to the signs, as well. Take a look to find yours or a partner's below.

Aries

Aries (March 21 to April 19), the ram, is the first sign of the zodiac, blazing a trail of fire. Aries are courageous, natural-born leaders that aren't afraid of competition. They possess a determined and confident nature, and tend to be multi-taskers who excel at physical challenges, as they enjoy staying active in mind and body.

Taurus

Earthly Taurus (April 20 to May 20), the bull, brings grounding and stability to a chart. Reliable, trustworthy, and responsible, Taurus has a realistic perspective. Taureans tend to spare no expense when it comes to beautification and comfort, as they place a high value on self-care. They are known for their resolution, and it's hard to change their minds or hearts once they're made up.

Gemini

Gemini (May 21 to June 20), the twins, can seem to have two sides, as they are multidimensional thinkers and creators. They tend to be either be curious, gentle, and affectionate or serious and restless (or sometimes all of the above). Geminis are quick learners, as well.

Cancer

Cancer (June 21 to July 22), the crab, is deeply sensitive, intuitive, and highly imaginative. Cancers can empathize easily, and tend to make loyal partners. They are known for keeping those they love close and place great value on friends, family, and home life.

Leo
Leo (July 23 to August 22), the lion, has a courageous heart of gold. Leos are warmhearted protectors who are generous, playful, and passionate. This cheerful sign relishes attention, and delights in a good party or gathering. Leos tend to possess a ton of confidence, along with a healthy sense of humor, so they can laugh with you, even if the joke is on them.

Virgo
Virgo (August 23 to September 22), the virgin, has an unmatched beauty, along with a meticulous eye for detail. Methodical, analytical, and practical, Virgos tend to relish planning and executing everything from work to personal affairs. This sign, like the name suggests, is endowed with natural innocence and sense of wonder.

Libra
Libra (September 23 to October 22), the scales of justice, is a peaceful ally and trusted friend. Libra people will never choose sides, and they like to maintain harmony. Always surrounded by friends, this sign enjoys company. Libras tend to be balanced, gracious, and diplomatic, and they delight in the beauty of life and the material world.

Scorpio
Scorpio (October 23 to November 21), the scorpion, asserts great determination (to the point of obsession). Intense, resourceful, and passionate, those born under this sign are fearless in the face of obstacles. The moody yet magnetic scorpion can be unsettling to signs with a light and airy demeanor. It cuts through superficiality to learn what moves your soul.

Sagittarius

Sagittarius (November 22 to December 21), the archer, is never in one place for long. Their ambitious sense of adventure is in a category of its own, as they are natural freedom lovers. Optimistic, intellectual, and hilarious, these spontaneous and funny philosophers are popular in a crowd, as their energy naturally attracts lots of smiles and laughter.

Capricorn

Capricorn (December 22 to January 19), the horned goat, brings in sensibility and practicality. Hardworking Capricorns can come across as serious in nature, because they are masters of self-control and discipline. Although they can be the pretty harsh on themselves, this sign is an excellent business partner and loyal friend.

Aquarius

Aquarius (January 20 to February 18), the Water Bearer, is definitely the esoteric one of the bunch. Celebrating all things unique, artistic, and unconventional, this sign is no stranger to the strange. With a sharp mind, the intellectual yet dreamy Aquarius is concerned with humanity and cares deeply about creating a better future for us all.

Pisces

Pisces (February 19 to March 20), the fish, are trustworthy allies, friends, and lovers. Caring, sensitive, and intuitive, Pisces are the selfless healers of the zodiac. This sign feels before it thinks and possesses a deep, creative well and emotional capacity. Gentle and compassionate, Pisces often understand you before you understand yourself.

THE 4 ELEMENTS

The four elements—water, earth, fire, and air—govern three signs apiece, and they play a huge role in the classification and predictability of each sign. These are the foundations through which individual predispositions are born. The elements highlight behavioral patterns, specific attributes, and tendencies of a sign.

The appearance of each element in your chart denotes your elemental balance. If you get a sense for the elemental relationship of a sign, you can reasonably understand proclivities and traits within it, and how certain signs behave together. Signs with the same element possess natural compatibility because they understand one another easily, as do air and fire and earth and water. Because your chart contains the placements of all the planets, you contain all of the elements within you. Individually, you can get a sense of your elemental balance by seeing how many placements you have in certain signs (especially your big three).

Fire

The fire signs are Aries, Leo, and Sagittarius. Fire rules the first, fifth, and ninth houses of the zodiac. Fire is a transformational element and leads the elements in intensity and flair for drama. This element is known for its spontaneity, excitability, and passion. Fire signs bring fun to any situation, as their enthusiasm is unmatched. People with dominant fire signs are unafraid of confrontation and possess a natural confidence.

Earth

The earth signs are Taurus, Virgo, and Capricorn. Earth rules the second, sixth, and tenth houses of the zodiac. Earth is a stabilizing element, and tends to be grounding and nurturing in its essence. The earth signs possess a strong inner wisdom and intellect. They take every chance to celebrate the beauty in the world but are also pragmatic, thoughtful, and hardworking. Like the ground below your feet, these signs take their commitments seriously and offer reliability and rootedness to those around them.

Water

The water signs are Cancer, Scorpio, and Pisces. Water rules the fourth, eighth, and twelfth houses of the zodiac. These signs have big emotions and can often sense what you're feeling, too. They tend to be intuitive and imaginative. Water signs are often misunderstood as moody because of their intensity, but they are really just sensitive.

Air

The air signs are Aquarius, Gemini, and Libra. Air rules the third, seventh, and eleventh houses of the zodiac. These signs are breezy, talkative, and intellectual. They thrive on the open exchange of ideas and love to innovate. The air signs are quick witted and rational, and don't spend much time being still, rather going where the wind takes them.

THE 3 MODALITIES

The three modalities in astrology are cardinal, fixed, and mutable. All the signs are assigned to one of these, so there are four signs per category. The modalities reveal a sign's approach to life. The groupings represent how the signs under them express their energy and react to various energetic inputs and circumstances.

The effect of the modalities compounds itself the more a specific modality shows up in your chart. For example, if your Sun, Moon, and rising signs are all fixed, you may experience difficulty moving forward, or making simple decisions can trip you up, because you tend to have a general inflexibility when it comes to change. Balance is more easily achieved within and without if you possess a blend of the three across your primary planets and in your overall chart. While we can't change how the modalities show up in our natal charts, we can learn to work with their energies.

Cardinal

The cardinal signs are Aries, Cancer, Libra, and Capricorn. They are pioneers and self-starters, so you'll find that they always keep themselves busy. There's never a dull moment for these signs, as they take initiative and like to keep moving forward at all costs. Cardinal signs don't want to wait if they don't have to, and they tend to go big or go home.

Fixed

The fixed signs are Taurus, Leo, Scorpio, and Aquarius. Fixed signs tend to be the stubborn group of the bunch. Once they make up their minds, they can be nearly impossible to change. They are deliberate, focused, and determined. If a fixed sign has their eye on a prize, you can bet they won't give up until they achieve success. It's not about winning, but about seeing something through to the end.

Mutable

The mutable signs are Gemini, Virgo, Sagittarius, and Pisces. Mutable signs are highly adaptable, which makes them excellent at navigating almost any curveball life throws at them. They go with the flow, but occasionally run into problems because they can also be relatively uncommitted.

THE MOON'S PHASES & YOU

Lunar energy represents the deep subconscious or inner realm of emotions. The Moon's phases mirror our own shifting states. The Moon has four major phases a month—new, waxing, full, and waning—repeating approximately once a month (every 29.5 days). Moon mapping can be beneficial for doing inner work. You can easily find a free lunar calculator online to determine the phase the Moon was in at the time of your birth.

The Moon phase you were born under reveal more intricate layers of your emotional self and subconscious operating system. The cycles originally held an agricultural purpose, and you can still meaningfully apply these to the cycles of your life. Take a look at the descriptions below to make sense of the Moon phases, which one you feel you are in now, and which you were born under. It may help connect the dots between your past, present, and future.

- New Moon: new beginnings, fresh starts, clarity, intention setting, and planting seeds

- Waxing crescent/gibbous Moon: motivation, momentum, creativity, and growth from a seed to a plant

- Full Moon: healing, charging, cleansing, and harvesting the plants

- Waning Moon: introspection, cycles ending, wisdom, and clearing crops for replanting

THE PLANETS

The planets are an important part of the cosmic puzzle and greatly influence the power dynamics within your astrological chart. While the big three define your individuality and core identity, the planets shape your daily behaviors and interactions with others. Each sign has a ruling planet, which describes the influential affinity between the planet and sign in which it feels most at ease. Because there are only nine planets, some planets rule more than one sign. The Sun and Moon are considered luminary bodies, but are included in the planetary groupings.

The inner planets (Mercury, Venus, Mars, the Sun, and the Moon) are considered your personal planets. They are close to Earth, and revolve around the Sun relatively quickly, passing rapidly through the zodiac. The outer planets (Jupiter, Saturn, Uranus, Neptune, and Pluto) are farther away and move very slowly. For example, Jupiter takes about twelve years to orbit the Sun. Therefore, these outer planets tend to shape generations instead of individual identity. They represent external influences and hold indirect effects on broad, collective themes you may encounter.

The Sun

The Sun is the luminary body that showcases your ego and personal power. It rules in fiery Leo, and all the other planets orbit around it. The Sun represents who you are at your core, and what fulfills you above all else.

The Moon

A deep self-reflective well, the Moon is the luminary body that represents your private, unexpressed thoughts and feelings. This lunar celestial satellite rules over watery Cancer, acting like a security blanket, allowing you to feel safe and nourished.

Mercury

Mercury is the planet in the solar system with the smallest orbit around the Sun. It governs the transfer of ideas and communication. This planet rules the signs of Gemini and Virgo, both of which tend to cruise the intellectual superhighway at record speeds. Your placement here determines how your inner philosopher teaches and preaches your worldly experiences.

Venus

With a 243-day orbit around the Sun, Venus is a champion of love, romance, and creature comforts. Venus rules two signs as well—Taurus and Libra. These signs value self-care, beauty, and sensuality. Placements here influence how you celebrate yourself and derive pleasure.

Mars

Mars revolves around the Sun every 687 days, and it governs fiery Aries. Named after the god of war, its energy is ambitious, confident, and somewhat competitive. Passion, purpose, and planning are born from the fires that ignite under this sign.

Jupiter

Jupiter, which revolves around the Sun every twelve years, rules Sagittarius. This is the planet of opportunity, and its placement in your chart signals where your luck lies. Eternally optimistic, this planet signals invincibility, expansion, and growth.

Saturn

Saturn, which makes a lap around the Sun every twenty-nine years, is considered cosmic law enforcement. This planet rules over Capricorn. Because of its long orbit, this planet only comes around a few times per lifetime, and when it does, it signals complete reorganization of foundational systems, new challenges, and lessons pointing to understanding our limitations.

Uranus

Uranus orbits the Sun once every eighty-four years. Uranus rules Aquarius, and due to its long orbital track, brings revolutionary vibes to each generation it splashes across. This planet feels radical, progressive, and intellectual. Placements here involve big societal shifts and technological advancements.

Neptune

Revolving round the Sun once every 165 years, Neptune is a planet of dreams and spirituality. It rules over watery Pisces and typically ushers in evolutionary change. Placement here evokes imagination, transcendence, and dissolving of boundaries/realities. When this planet shows up, expect radical shift.

Pluto

Pluto, with its 248-year orbit of the Sun, is a deep internal well of the soul. Pluto rules in watery Scorpio, and its name comes from the god of the underworld. Plutonian energy refuses to be ignored; it calls in shadow work, ushering in intense transformation and harnessing the power of the light to cut through your darkest challenges and fears.

THE 12 HOUSES

The zodiac is divided into twelve houses, each ruled by its own zodiac sign. Think about the astrological houses as the stage you are playing on at any given time. They are thought to be areas in which much of your energy and attention will be spent. Some astrologers believe the "empty houses"—houses without planets in them in your natal chart—are areas in which you've already achieved mastery (perhaps in a past life), so your lessons are now showing up in other areas of your chart.

The planets and signs play in the different houses as they move through their transits, lighting up your chart with different energies. Through your unique placements, you can obtain valuable information on how, when, and what kind of decisions will best benefit you at any given time. The first six houses are the personal houses, while the last six deal with interpersonal issues. The zodiac begins with the first house (the self) and goes counterclockwise around as it expands out to society and beyond. The houses, their rulers, and traits are as follows:

First House (Aries): "firsts"—first impressions, the self and appearance, and new starts

Second House (Taurus): money, possessions, self-esteem, personal resources, and mothers

Third House (Gemini): communication, community, siblings, and mental activity

Fourth House (Cancer): home, foundation, privacy, security, and parents

Fifth House (Leo): creativity, expression, drama, romance, play, and fun

Sixth House (Virgo): work, service, health, fitness, and self-improvement

Seventh House (Libra): partnerships, marriage and business, and relationship matters

Eighth House (Scorpio): death, birth, sex, transformation, investments, and inheritances

Ninth House (Sagittarius): travel, expansion, adventure, and foreign languages

Tenth House (Capricorn): career, public image, achievements, awards, and fathers

Eleventh House (Aquarius): aspirations, friends/teams, society, technology, and surprises

Twelfth House (Pisces): endings, spiritual life, imagination, and the subconscious mind

ASTROLOGY IS A LIFE-CHANGING PRACTICE

Astrology can be as basic or as complicated as you make it, so go easy on yourself, especially if you are just dipping your toes in the water for the first time. Some people make astrology an entire career, as there are many systems, elements, applications, and interpretations to learn about. However, you can begin using the knowledge in this book right now to improve your life in simple ways. As you focus on the changes you want to make and begin using the exercises, your inner landscape will start to shift. Be patient, as it takes time to observe the transformation, and above all else, have fun with it!

Combining Astrology with Crystals Will Help You Level Up

In the next section, you'll be learning about crystals, and how they can be used as tools to create and sustain beauty, meaning, and intentionality in your life. Leading a conscious life means that you feel fulfilled and in alignment, connected to your life's purpose. Both astrology and crystals are powerful tools for working through your own healing and life mission. By using these tools in tandem, you can realize real change as you open up to new perspectives and spiritual gifts. These tools can help you remember who you are and what you came here to do. Trust the process. You are on the right path!

KEY TAKEAWAYS

In this chapter, we covered everything you need to know to get started on your cosmic journey into astrology. You are now well equipped to explore the vast subject of astrology and your own relationship to the starry skies. Here's a quick recap:

- Astrology has a rich history, with many branches and interpretations. We'll be using Western (tropical) astrology in this book.

- To get started, you'll want to pull a birth (natal) chart, and you can do this easily from any astrology website with a free calculator.

- The signs, elements, planets, and houses all interact with one another to deliver a broad picture of how you relate, respond to, and interact with the world around you.

- If you get confused, stick to your big three placements (Sun, Moon, and rising/ascendant signs) until you get the hang of things.

- Your personal zodiac is not meant to tell the future but simply reflects what your best-case scenarios could look like and offers higher perspective to help you navigate challenges. Use it as a tool to open up the mystery areas of your life as you explore, enjoy, and share.

CHAPTER 2

CRYSTALS 101

I n this chapter, we'll take a look at crystals and learn more about these natural treasures that come from the earth. We will define what exactly a crystal is, as well as how to select the perfect one for your practice. We'll touch on responsible sourcing, myths and misconceptions, and how crystals can enhance your life. This book will suggest crystals to use as part of your zodiac exercises, providing background on their origins and uses so you can get to know them more intimately.

We're going to review important foundational information for beginners, including how to connect with and care for your crystals. Properly caring for your stones can aid in keeping their energies clear so your stones do their job more efficiently. There is so much to learn about crystals, so let's get started.

WHAT ARE CRYSTALS?

Crystals act as a beautiful physical reminder to mind our energy while also giving us access to their own special energies. Crystals can also keep us on track, as they aid in setting intentions. Unlike goals, which are focused on future-based outcomes, intentions are about the present moment. Crystals additionally can connect you more deeply to your purpose and spiritual path.

Crystals possess a specific structure and stable, unchanging energy pattern, which gives each a unique vibration or frequency. Crystalline solids are arranged in highly ordered atomic, molecular, or ionic structures called **lattices,** and are normally classified by their shape. They can be found raw and unpolished, or they can be cut and chiseled. Different than gemstones, which are classified by their chemical makeup and can be organic or inorganic, crystals are pure organic materials. They may include **mineral** deposits (naturally occurring solids with a specific chemical composition) that are different from the crystal material itself. They can range widely in price, color, and size.

A BRIEF HISTORY OF CRYSTALS

Crystals have always held a special place in humanity's heart. Many cultures around the world used crystals for their healing properties, including the ancient Greeks. In fact, they attributed many properties to the stones while naming a great many of the stones we know of today. The word *crystal* originates from a Greek word for ice; clear quartz was said to resemble water that had frozen so deeply that it would forever remain in solid form. Today, more everyday people are tuning in to nature's crystal gifts for personal and spiritual expansion. As human consciousness evolves, the ancient-future technologies and healing tools of the past are making a huge comeback.

WHERE DO CRYSTALS COME FROM?

Crystals grow naturally in the Earth's crust, or they can be manufactured. Natural crystals from form through a process called crystallization. Lattice structures begin to form when liquid or condensation is heated and then cooled and the remaining molecules stabilize, hardening into specific patterns. As more atoms join, a uniform and repetitive pattern begins to take shape. Hard, soft, silky, sharded, and shimmering—crystals each have their own special structure, mood, and personality. Crystals are diverse and prevalent in nature and can vary from the minuscule to hundreds of pounds.

You might be lucky enough to find a naturally occurring crystal in nature, although most need to be mined. Crystals can be found anywhere on earth, including up to 25 miles below its surface. This is precisely why the growing your own crystals is gaining in popularity. Many jewelry companies are creating crystalline pieces to save the time and money, while avoiding mining's adverse effects. Manufactured crystals are often made in a lab, using a vaporization and distillation technique, and are virtually indistinguishable from nature-made crystals if they are done well. They may be heat-treated and dyed to make them look like their "natural" counterparts, and often there's no good way to tell. You'll want to determine which type of crystal you are looking at before purchasing, as how they were created can play a role in the stone's energetic feel.

RESPONSIBLE SOURCING

In a crystal's journey from its harvest to you, it touches many hands and travels many miles, picking up energy along the way. When I started my healing journey, I couldn't name a single person who was involved in crystal mining or trading. Since then, I've invested a lot of time and energy into making the appropriate contacts to ensure the earth isn't being depleted and that the energy of the stones I buy/collect are of the absolute highest vibration.

The crystal industry has been impacted negatively by mining practices, which can damage the ground in which the crystals grow. Additionally, miners often suffer poor working conditions, especially in less-developed countries. You can source your stones responsibly by looking for sellers who support local families with mining land or own/prospect small-batch local mines. Asking questions like "Who has collected, packed, and profited from this crystal?" will help you ensure no harmful practices were involved in a crystal's procurement. You may end up paying a bit more for ethically sourced crystals, but you'll know that know that your crystal didn't result in the exploitation or suffering of the earth or other people. From an energetic standpoint, you'll end up with a crystal with a higher vibration.

CRYSTALS CAN ENHANCE YOUR LIFE

Crystals can create huge shifts in your life, if you allow them to. The best part about crystals is that even if you don't own a specific crystal, you may still tune in to its energetic properties remotely through meditation. Just imagine yourself sitting with whatever stone you has an energetic blueprint on which you want to call. If you have the crystal with you physically, its energy will begin to radiate out to your room or environment right away. Crystals can be helpful in many ways. Following are a few of those.

Heal Mind, Body & Spirit

Your mind, body, and spiritual layers are all interconnected. Sometimes, it's difficult to access one if another is blocked or holding negative energy patterns. Crystals enable you to reconnect to your mind, body, and spirit to clear blocks and harness your highest potential. They do this in subtle ways often over time. You may notice your patience increasing, less pain in tender areas of your body, and an increase in your spiritual curiosity. Just remember, sometimes healing can be messy before it feels beautiful. Embrace the change, and welcome in healing in all its forms.

Shift & Focus Your Energy

When you are feeling stuck, crystals can help to shift your energy. They help to bring mental awareness and allow you to focus your energy and build your mindfulness practice as though you are building a muscle. It takes time and patience to consistently refocus your energy. Give yourself a chance to become distracted, then refocus and see how much simpler it gets each time.

Relieve Negative Feelings

Negative feelings are simply stuck emotions of a lower vibration that are trapped inside the body. Sometimes, we need assistance removing these lower energies, as they can become stagnant and form "dis-ease" (the state of being in illness). Negative feelings can include anger, jealousy, silent rage, childhood or adult trauma, sadness, grief, distress, and fear. These lower vibrations may not dissipate in one day, but crystals will help to slowly raise the vibration in your body so that they aren't as disruptive. Eventually, these feelings will turn into more positive ones, as you continue your awareness practice (daily if possible).

Help You Set Intentions

Intention setting is a practice of stating what you intend to accomplish before doing so. It is an act that puts into motion the creation of your dreams, goals, and desires. The simple act of drawing focus to your intention begins to set up its energetic blueprint. Using crystals can help you bring your intention into being by setting up the blueprint of your highest vibrational alignment and aspirations. The best way to do this is to use crystals when you are in a clear headspace and without distractions or interruptions.

MYTHS & MISCONCEPTIONS ABOUT CRYSTALS

There are a few things about crystals that are commonly misunderstood. One of the biggest misconceptions about crystals is that you need to be "new age" to work with them. While crystals definitely expand your conscious awareness, you do not need to have any background in the metaphysical to benefit from their energy. Crystals are for anyone willing to approach their own healing with an open heart and mind.

Another misconception is that crystals will somehow work better if they are more expensive. Your stone may be pretty or unattractive, pricey or free, large or small. None of these factors are important, nor do they affect the way the crystal works. Finding the right stone involves careful selection and a unique and invaluable bond between you and your crystal.

Caring for your stone is something else I hear confusion around. Cleansing and storing your crystals properly are important steps that should not be overlooked. You'll want to make sure you do this every time, especially between personal use and use on others. If you aren't cleansing your crystals, they can hold old energies and stop their healing properties may diminish over time.

CHOOSING CRYSTALS THAT ARE RIGHT FOR YOU

Get quiet and listen to the crystals that are asking for your attention when choosing the stone that's right for you. Pay attention to which ones want to go home with you or seem to be passing you telepathic messages. You may find crystals call out to you when you are in need of specific healing, or if your chakra energy is low. Usually, the ones you are naturally attracted to are the ones that are going to be most complimentary for you at that moment.

Beginners often gravitate toward chakra sets, rainbow-colored stones to represent all the energies in the physical body. You may also enjoy clear or smoky quartz, as these are easy to find in any crystal store, more cost-conscious, and great for all types of meditation and grid work (the use of crystals around the house in grid patterns or stacked them together for charging a large area). In this book, you'll be introduced to crystals that correspond to your personal astrology.

PRACTICAL ADVICE FOR USING YOUR CRYSTALS

There's not really a wrong way to connect with crystals. The best thing to do is to intend to connect by making time to sit with your new crystal once it comes into your hands. Simply by holding them during quiet time or meditation, they will begin to improve your energy and attune you to their crystalline consciousness. Many people choose to place them around their rooms, homes, or office space to receive their benefits. You can even program your crystals for specific functions, some of which we'll practice in the exercises in this book.

Try holding your crystals one at a time to get a feel for their unique energetic signatures. Discover each crystal's unique essence through direct connection. Try placing them in a handbag, backpack, or pocket so that your crystal can work for you over time. I love bringing my important crystals to sacred sites, so before traveling, I ask, "Who wants to come along?" and always wrap a few up for the ride. Crystals usually enjoy "talking" to one another, so they enjoy being grouped together. Others prefer to stand alone as a centerpiece in your collection, by your bedside, or under your pillow while you sleep.

CARING FOR YOUR CRYSTALS

As soon as you bring your new crystal baby home, give it a good cleanse. Cleansing can include smudging the crystal with aromatic plants and/or running it under cool water. Use care when placing your crystals in or around water, like in gem elixirs or mineral baths. Some crystals aren't to be around water at all, as they may crack, dissolve, release toxic minerals, or rust. In general, anything under 5 on the **Mohs hardness scale** (a 1-to-10 measure of a mineral's hardness and resistance to

CREATING A CRYSTAL GRID OR ALTAR SPACE

A crystal grid is an arrangement of crystals, placed in a specific order or shape, to amplify the crystals' energies and hold the energy within a space for a particular intention or purpose. You can use any combination of crystals inside a grid, and a grid can be simple or complex, depending on its purpose. I enjoy using crystals that feel like they belong together like rose quartz (love), amethyst (protection), and clear quartz (amplification). If you aren't sure which go with which, let your intuition guide you. In general, clear quartz is always used inside a grid to increase the power and energy of the formation. All terminated points (ends) should be pointing to the inside of the grid or along the outside lines. A master stone is placed either in the center of the grid to beam energy to the rest of the space, or outside of the grid to bring energy into the arrangement. The energy will stay for about one to four weeks, and you can refresh the grid or cleanse it as needed.

You can place your new grid on an altar space or sacred area of intention. To make any space an altar, make sure it's undisturbed and clear of anything else. You can place special meaningful items on your altar, such as crystals, shells, healing herbs, flowers, candles, or a recent oracle/tarot card pull. You may also consider putting a vision board up on or near your altar, or a few pictures that are special to you.

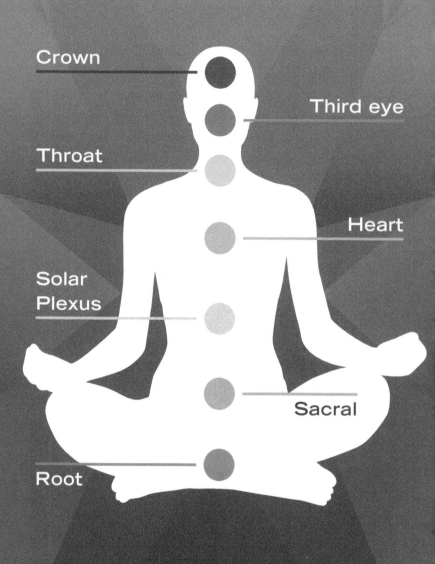

scratching, with a diamond as a 10) should be kept out of water altogether. This includes crystals like selenite, pyrite, desert rose, fluorite, and kyanite, to name a few. All the exercises in this book are designed with crystal safety in mind.

To charge your crystals, you can place them outside on the earth under the moonlight. You may opt to do this on a full or new Moon as part of a ritual or ceremony, but any night will do. You may also consider day-charging your crystals. While some crystals love the Sun, others (like amethyst) should avoid direct sunlight whenever possible. You could also place your crystals on an altar space and/or within a **crystal grid** (an arrangement of crystals) to amplify their energy. We'll take a closer look at how to create an altar space shortly.

THE CONNECTION BETWEEN CRYSTALS & CHAKRAS

You have seven main chakras, or energy centers, that run the full length of your body. The primary chakras, in ascending order, are root, sacral, solar plexus, heart, throat, third eye, and crown. The chakras allow energy to pass in and out of your physical body and auric field, each corresponding to a color and frequency range, while governing certain bodily systems and functions.

I highly recommend beginning to work with a basic chakra set of crystals for all healing work, as this is the easiest way to bring alignment and raise the frequency of your chakras to boost your body's natural ability to heal itself. For instance, if you feel disconnected to your purpose and personal power, working with a solar plexus stone like citrine will help to bring this energy back into connection and resonance. You can do this for each chakra, as needed, to help restore balance and vital energy.

THE HEALING POWER
OF CRYSTALS

It may take some time to become comfortable using your understanding to work with the crystals. Crystals are so personal, as their energies react slightly differently to everyone. One crystal that resonates for your friend may not for you. You are free to choose a different selection than an exercise calls for based on what feels right to you. Crystals can help you connect with yourself, improve the way you experience the world, and improve your life. You may sense your relationships with your crystals and with yourself changing as you go through your mindfulness exercises, and that's perfectly natural. Embrace all changes lovingly.

Combining Crystals with Astrology Will Expand Your Power

Both astrology and crystals complement and enhance one another in big ways. Using these together will give you new perspectives on your life, opening the doors of destiny with knowledge and empowerment. You'll start to notice new levels of awareness as things around you shift, all in service to your highest vibration. You'll grow on all levels, as your new access to spiritual realms will help you discover who you are meant to be in this lifetime. We will be exploring this connection even more deeply in the coming chapters, so feel free to take as much time as you need to practice and feel into the exercises.

KEY TAKEAWAYS

In this chapter, we covered everything you need to know to get started on your crystal journey. You are well equipped as you start to explore all there is to know about the magical world of crystals. Here's a quick recap of what was covered:

- There are many types of crystals, classified by their structural differences (called lattices) on a molecular and atomic level. They are different than minerals, stones, and gemstones.

- Ethical sourcing of your crystals is important. It affects the energy of the stones, and this is particularly imperative if you are using the crystals for healing.

- Start with a chakra set of crystals if you are confused where to begin so you can work with your own energy centers for clearing and balance.

- Crystals can help you focus your energy while connecting your mind, body, and spirit, opening you up to higher spiritual gateways.

- You will connect best with your crystals as you form a personal bond with your stone, which happens over time. Take the time to be quiet and listen. If nothing else, the crystal energy will work on the space it is placed in, quietly raising the vibrations in the background until you are ready to uncover its full magic.

PART II

DEEPEN YOUR KNOWLEDGE OF THE SIGNS & CRYSTALS

T he zodiac is more than the planetary movements we observe in the known universe. Its study has become a pursuit of character analysis and guide to self-development. This is a path of uncovering the building blocks of our lives.

Crystals, also formed over thousands of years, help us to navigate the ocean of astrology. We use them to aid us in overcoming obstacles, clearing uncomplimentary energies (energies that drain the life force), directing attention and focus, and cultivating intentional living practices. In the upcoming section, you'll get a closer look at the twelve zodiac signs, as well as the thirty-six crystals used in the practices in this book. The crystals are each paired with an exercise specific to the Sun, Moon, and rising signs of each zodiac. The work you do here may help you to see and know things about yourself that speak to the mysteries of your own soul's higher calling.

CHAPTER 3

ZODIAC PROFILES

W̲e will look at each of the signs in this chapter, examining traits, qualities, elements, planets, and characteristics that make each unique. As we go through the signs, you'll notice we begin with Aries, which is seen as the start of the astrological year (versus the calendar year). The Sun moving into Aries signals the start of the spring equinox in the northern hemisphere, and as the season gives bloom to new life, so begins another Sun cycle.

The dates of the Sun's transits change ever so slightly according to the Sun's actual movement, from our perspective here on Earth. We may sense these slight changes, yet the signs and houses remain fixed in their positions to create stability within the cycles of our own lives. As these forces work within us, we are able to better understand our connection to the cosmos, Earth, one another, and ourselves.

ARIES (MARCH 21 – APRIL 19)

A new zodiac cycle begins with the ingress (moving into) of the Sun into Aries. The first house of the zodiac, Aries is a cardinal fire sign, ruled by Mars and named after the god of war. It is represented by a charging ram, which puts everything it has into the energy of the moment. Aries represent the *I am* presence. They are pioneers who like to go first, and they are the warriors of the zodiac. The associated crystals for Aries are carnelian, druzy quartz, and tiger's eye.

Aries Sun: In the eyes of others, Aries Suns are courageous leaders who move quickly to accomplish challenges without hesitation. This can be viewed as aggressive or reactionary, though this form of directness only needs to be tempered in the right way to shine.

Aries Moon: Aries Moon positions are satisfied by excitement and spontaneity. Always the overachiever, they usually get what they want. They may be impulsive or impatient, so short-term projects are best.

Aries Rising: This placement is unendingly enthusiastic, sassy, bold and flexible, though they may find challenges finishing what they started. They may lean toward competitiveness (though often self-directed) and will need to watch out for reckless errors or skipping steps.

TAURUS (APRIL 20 – MAY 20)

Lovely Taurus, a fixed earth sign, welcomes us to the second house of the zodiac. Ruled by Venus, the planet of love, Taurus the bull is all about beauty, loving connection, and sensuality. Taureans are naturally grounded individuals who enjoy consistency, stability, and security. Patient, conscientious, and hardworking, Taureans know how to get a job done right. They tend to resent change. True to their stubborn-as-a-bull nature, once they have an idea in their head, it can be rather hard to convince them otherwise. The associated crystals for Taurus are smoky quartz, celestite, and jade.

Taurus Sun: This bull is straightforward and often goes headfirst into opportunities, seeing them out to longevity as they are builders by nature. Some may call them obstinate, while others may see them as dedicated and willing to nurture any project to fruition.

Taurus Moon: Deeply connected to the physical world, this Earth lover is a guardian of nature and all beings. This Moon placement is extremely sensual and appreciates soothing smells, tastes, and touch.

Taurus Rising: Pragmatic and loyal, this placement makes a great partner or best friend. They do not like being pushed or rushed into things. Their devotion can border possessiveness with partners because of how strongly they love.

GEMINI (MAY 21 – JUNE 20)

In the third house of the zodiac, we find Gemini, the celestial twins, who are both separate yet connected. This mutable placement is ruled by the god and planet Mercury. This sparkly air sign is a thinker by nature and thrives in social situations in which they can feel fully expressed in mind and voice. Geminis are observant and curious but may be viewed as slightly scatterbrained. Handle your Gemini with care, as this sign has two sides, and you never know which one you'll get. They represent polarity in the zodiac. The associated crystals for Gemini are Lemurian quartz, fluorite, and blue sodalite.

Gemini Sun: Adaptable and fluid, this master of disguise is unpredictable and can embody a number of personas depending on the situation. A Gemini Sun is up for an intellectual challenge, and its dual nature means it covers twice the ground in half the time by multitasking.

Gemini Moon: This placement represents a pinnacle of communication and the exchange of ideas. Gemini Moons need a constant stream of mental stimulation or they can get easily bored. Don't be surprised if they seem cold, as they compartmentalize their feelings to make sense of the world.

Gemini Rising: Fascinated by the world, Gemini Moon embraces the ebb and flow of life freely and relatively unattached. Flitting from here to there, they might be considered flaky. To them, being trapped by concrete obligations feels suffocating.

CANCER (JUNE 21 – JULY 22)

Cancer, the crab, is deceptively soft on the inside once you get past their shell. This cardinal water sign sits in the fourth house of the zodiac, ruled by Moon. This sign is quite the homebody, as the crab carries its home on its back. Cancers are traditional and protective by nature, fiercely guarding over their family affairs. Sensitive, emotional, and intuitive, they prefer to feel their way through situations, rather than using an intellectual approach. The corresponding crystals for Cancer are chrysocolla, larimar, and peach moonstone.

Cancer Sun: The crab moves back and forth between intuition's deep waters and the safety of grounded shoreline. Highly sensitive, the Cancer Sun craves its personal sanctuary from the physical and emotional world, and has keen perception to navigate between the two. The crab Sun is imaginative, gentle, and nurturing.

Cancer Moon: The crab's Moon placement denotes extra sensitivity to stress (and all areas of life). They can be moody, impractical, and demanding, so this sign needs more love and reassurance than most. Establishing boundaries is important for cancer Moons.

Cancer Rising: Vulnerability and intimacy are their strong suits, and showing this side can help others to break out of their shy hermit shell, too. Cancer rising is a nurturing caregiver.

LEO (JULY 23 – AUGUST 22)

Leo the lion roars into the fifth house of the zodiac with a commanding presence. This fixed fire sign is ruled by the Sun. The lion prides itself on being able to make practical decisions under fire, for the benefit of many. They rule compassionately, with a generous and bighearted nature. Leos demand respect and often have a flair for the dramatic. They don't mind being the center of attention. They are the fiercely loving leader in the zodiac. The crystals associated with Leo are citrine, sunstone, and amazonite.

Leo Sun: A confident leader, Leo Sun is usually directing others for some worthy cause. Practical and organized, people naturally trust Leos in this position. They are generally positive, enthusiastic, and supportive.

Leo Moon: Despite being king or queen of the jungle, Leo Moon is a sensitive soul. They aren't fragile by any means, but their ego can easily bruise. These placements respond best to devoted partners and friends who understand their fierce yet loving nature.

Leo Rising: In this placement, Leo rising is self-assured, passionate, and proud. If they are not mindful, they can come across as overbearing or pushy. They are adored and loved by many, and have an easy time making friends and keeping them for a lifetime.

VIRGO (AUGUST 23 – SEPTEMBER 22)

Virgo, the mutable earth sign, ushers us into the sixth house of the zodiac. Ruled by the speedy planet Mercury, Virgo is represented by the Virgin or the goddess of wheat and agriculture. Virgos are the realists of the zodiac, and tend to be orderly, conservative, and rather analytical. Fastidious and detail oriented, they are considered the worriers of the zodiac. They have a graceful demeanor and highly sensitive nervous systems. The corresponding crystals for Virgo are rose quartz, lepidolite, and apophyllite.

Virgo Sun: The Sun in this placement confers grounded structure. This sign needs to review lots of evidence to make changes. Lovers of beauty and nature, Virgo Suns are caring and heart-centered.

Virgo Moon: Perfectionists by nature, this placement could best benefit from getting out of its own way, and trying on more magical thinking.

Virgo Rising: This placement is excellent at planning and executing practical matters. However, Virgo rising are often nit-pickers and should be careful to not be overly critical or project their worries onto others.

LIBRA (SEPTEMBER 23 – OCTOBER 22)

The cardinal Libra is represented by the scales of justice, signifying balance. This air sign is the halfway point in the astrological cycle and sits in the seventh house of the zodiac. Ruled by Venus, Libras are lovers, not fighters. Charismatic, charming, and agreeable, this sign is quite magnetic and knows how to work a crowd. They strive for equanimity and are the diplomats of the zodiac. Libras are rarely caught speaking ill of anyone. They care a lot about how others view them. The associated crystals of Libra are moonstone, agate, and selenite.

Libra Sun: The Libra Sun is concerned with finding harmony, symmetry, and beauty. They work toward building a world that supports others and often think in terms of the collective. They approach problems objectively and compromise or adjust to ensure a fair outcome for all.

Libra Moon: This placement enjoys beautification of all sorts, deriving much emotional satisfaction from their creations. These artists are graceful and easygoing charmers who can occasionally get stuck in their own fantasies and procrastinations.

Libra Rising: Understanding and good-natured, this sign is often the one that their friends go to for advice and solace. Always ready to lend an ear, and their well-contemplated two cents, this peacekeeper is socially adept, optimistic, and cheerful.

SCORPIO (OCTOBER 23 – NOVEMBER 21)

♏ Piercing Scorpio is situated in the eighth house, which is ruled over by the planet of death and regeneration, Pluto. Before Pluto was discovered in the 1930s, Mars (the god of war) was the ruler of Scorpio. This fixed water sign is represented by the scorpion, which is always poised to strike should a threat come their way. Intense, mysterious, and powerful, this water element can feel more like fire, lending to the penetrative way it transforms all situations. Scorpio charms their way to your inner realms. The associated crystals for Scorpio are garnet, serpentine, and obsidian.

Scorpio Sun: Dominant and somewhat intimidating, the Sun in this placement may feel brooding and deeply intense. Scorpio Suns don't waste time with frivolous small talk. They tend to scrutinize everything in a deliberate manner with unyielding ferocity.

Scorpio Moon: Scorpion Moon is comfortable pushing past limits within themselves and in others. This placement can come off as aggressive and somewhat secretive. They feel emotionally satisfied keeping their own affairs private, while they obsess over the secrets of the universe.

Scorpio Rising: Scorpio ascendant rises to the occasion, like a phoenix from the ashes. Scorpio recognizes what must die off to be reborn. This placement is seriously committed to their cause and has quite the rebellious streak.

SAGITTARIUS (NOVEMBER 22 – DECEMBER 21)

The mutable fire sign Sagittarius is ruled by the expansive planet of Jupiter. Fun and freedom loving, this optimistic sign presides over the ninth house of the zodiac. Sagittarius is represented by the centaur archer, the half-human, half-horse creature who shoots a bow and arrow through the heavens. A courageous dreamer, Sagittarians believe absolutely anything is possible, and they are here to prove it. This sign represents higher learning, and they can often be found reading multiple books at once. They are the travelers of the zodiac. The associated crystals for Sagittarius are pyrite, labradorite, and red jasper.

Sagittarius Sun: An enthusiastic explorer, this Sun placement loves to travel and is always on the move. They tend to be impulsive, and may come and go without much explanation.

Sagittarius Moon: The Moon in this placement is rather independent and individualistic, making them the popular one in a crowd. They are versatile and adaptive in almost all situations, and emotionally satisfied when they are free to roam.

Sagittarius Rising: Always the popular one, the comical Sag rising inspires others to be more lighthearted and carefree. On occasion, they can suffer from foot-in-mouth syndrome, but generally, their sense of humor can save them.

CAPRICORN (DECEMBER 22 – JANUARY 19)

The Capricorn is a mythological sea-goat creature with the body of a goat and tail of a fish. Studious Capricorn welcomes us into the tenth house of the zodiac, ruled by Saturn. This cardinal earth sign has a determined and serious demeanor, and they are highly reliable individuals. Methodical and persistent Capricorns always have a plan to get the job done and do so deliberately and with discipline. This sign is the boss of the zodiac and has a commanding, and rather unheeding, nature. The associated crystals for Capricorn are tourmaline, malachite, and clear quartz.

Capricorn Sun: Steady, dependable, and efficient, this Sun placement has a relentless drive to achieve. They are no strangers to hard work. They can come across as domineering and overbearing.

Capricorn Moon: This placement can be dominant and demanding, so the biggest challenge for them is to lighten up. Expressing their emotions and accessing vulnerability is not a strong suit for them.

Capricorn Rising: Stubborn at the core, Capricorn rising tends to find fulfillment accomplishing goals, but can be highly critical and judgmental if they catch you doing something "the wrong way."

AQUARIUS (JANUARY 20 – FEBRUARY 18)

The fixed sign Aquarius sits at the eleventh house of the zodiac, and rules the new age in which we are living (the Aquarian Age). Uranus guides progressive Aquarius, symbolized by the water bearer. Though this sign is connected to (and often associated with) water, this is a highly mental air sign. The Aquarian is forward-thinking, collaborative, and community-focused. They know change comes through the work of dismantling oppression, so they aren't afraid of revolution. Often concerned with the state and condition of humanity, this sign is the rebel and ambassador of change. The associated crystals for Aquarius are amethyst, turquoise, and aquamarine.

Aquarius Sun: Quirky and unique, this sign is always creating wherever they go. Ever the anarchist, they are natural-born leaders and are sure to cause a stir, as they are likely plotting the next coup. This placement can sometimes be unreliable due to its ever-changing and airy nature.

Aquarius Moon: Cool and somewhat detached, Aquarian Moons have a tendency to be difficult to understand and interact with. Their sharp mind and quick words redeem them for anyone willing to overlook their cold demeanor.

Aquarius Rising: Quite the artist, this placement is always creating some masterpiece. They are bright, entertaining, and accepting of others. What you see in yourself as a fault, Aquarius rising sees as your strength. They challenge the norms and, because of this, can be quite unruly and ungovernable.

PISCES (FEBRUARY 19 – MARCH 20)

Pisces the fish is a mutable water sign, ruled by the dreamy planet Neptune. Closing out the zodiac as the last sign in the twelfth house, this highly intuitive sign displays a level of unparalleled psychic mastery. This sign represents a full circle cycle through the zodiac, along with important lessons. The healers of the zodiac, they harness a high level of spirituality. Pisces are extremely sensitive souls particularly vulnerable to harsh words or rejection. They tend to float through their life as though in a dream. The associated crystals for Pisces are lapis, howlite, and black kyanite.

Pisces Sun: Selfless, compassionate, and empathetic, this healer is a true giver and will hold your heart with integrity.

They may suffer from a wounded ego over the smallest thing, but they will be there for you in a heartbeat.

Pisces Moon: The Piscean Moon placement can often be accused of being overly sensitive. Getting lots of alone time is of the highest benefit to them and helps them recharge.

Pisces Rising: Ever the people pleaser, Pisces ascendant is adaptable and fluid, tending to be quite self-sacrificing when it comes to personal relationships. They must take care not to be someone else's doormat by establishing strong boundaries.

CHAPTER 4

CRYSTAL PROFILES

T he crystals we will be working with were selected for their unique vibration and helpfulness in healing work. They are each special in their own way, carrying a specific frequency that, when paired with the exercises presented in this book, can yield powerful benefits. I have personally seen these crystals improve physical and mental health and open people up spiritually.

The crystals we will focus on in this section are organized by the twelve Sun, Moon, and rising signs, for a total of thirty-six crystals. We will go through each of the profiles according to the order in which they appear in the zodiac. Feel free to bookmark your favorites and come back to them if you are seeking to work with them outside the context of this book. The wisdom they have to share is channeled directly from the earth, and they love to share their wisdom.

CARNELIAN

True to its fire stone nature, Carnelian inspires, warms, and energizes. A bright red-orange with marbled banding, carnelians correspond to the sacral chakra and the sign of Aries. They represent passion, intimacy, connection, and creativity. They were considered a favorite among ancient Egyptian jewelry lapidaries because of their brilliant, gemmy appearance. Carnelians are a member of the quartz chalcedony family, primarily consisting of silicon dioxide and typically sold as polished pieces, as they are semiprecious. They can look cloudy in appearance with swirls of various oranges and reds.

Carnelians offer a wide variety of healing properties, including cleansing and purifying the blood, liver, and kidneys. This stone is thought to banish sorrow, and is commonly used in manifestation rituals, because it is a major attractor of energy. Used in womb healing and for healing the yin/yang connection within all beings, carnelians make superior stones for unlocking and balancing the sacral energies within. They can help to achieve balance and harmony, stimulate appetite, encourage sensuality, and connect you to your feelings in a way few crystals can.

DRUZY QUARTZ

Druzy quartz is one of the top stones for overall aura cleansing and stress relief. Druzy refers to a fine layer of glittering quartz crystallized on the surface (or inside) of a quartz-mineral. They are found everywhere in the world. Often, you'll need to crack open a big rock to find them, as they tend to hide inside the hollow cavity of other stones (such as agate geodes). Druzy is formed naturally when minerals are pulled to a crystal's surface and then cool, creating a sugar-like effect. It can be found in many shades and colors, with mineral **inclusions** (when a material is trapped inside during formation) and without.

Druzy quartz is associated with the higher chakras, such as the heart, throat, third eye, and crown chakras, and is connected to the zodiac sign of Aries. These crystals calm the emotional body, for one. You should work with druzy if you are experiencing sadness, grief, depression, or fear, as it will alleviate these lower vibrational energies. Druzy works on your whole aura, washing away negativity while promoting relaxation and stress relief. These stones are great to use when you are traveling because they remove unwanted energies you may have inadvertently picked up during your journey.

TIGER'S EYE

A powerful protector, tiger's eye is another member of the chalcedony mineral family, resembling a cat's or tiger's eye in appearance. With a smooth look that conceals any lattice structures, this stone shimmers with multidimensional complexity. It can be used for healing the lower chakras, including the solar plexus and sacral chakras. It represents optimism, good luck, confidence, and vitality, making it excellent for connecting with your presence and purpose. Associated with the sign of Aries, this stone carries the vibrations of both the Earth and the Sun, showcasing brilliant bands of yellow or brownish-gold hues throughout. Opaque in nature with an iridescent sheen, this stone is often found polished in varying shapes and sizes. Most of the tiger's eye comes from South Africa, Thailand, India, Brazil, and China.

Tiger's eye carries a grounding vibration that isn't always suitable for the extremely sensitive. It carries a duality to it, which can help you to see both sides to a situation to create positive outcomes. Calming fears and anxieties, tiger's eye boosts feelings of self-worth, especially during periods of change. It is thought to harmonize hormonal imbalances, as well.

SMOKY QUARTZ

Smoky quartz, true to its name, is a member of the quartz family, making it a powerful protection and grounding stone. Quartz, a hexagonal silica dioxide, is the most common and abundantly found mineral. Quartz comes in many colors, shapes, and sizes, and holds many practical uses. Smoky quartz is translucent, with a hazy or frosted tinge of light brown or black inside, giving it a smoky appearance. It can be found throughout the world but often comes from mining areas in Brazil, Africa, Australia, Switzerland, and the United States.

This stone is typically associated with the root chakra and the sign of Taurus because of its heavy, earthy feel. This stone is meant to connect you more to your *I am* presence, which helps establish your boundaries and stabilize any swirling energies. It aids in calming fears and lifting sadness, bringing you back to your center. Working with smoky quartz has somewhat of a detox effect, as it helps dispel negative energies. This is an excellent stone for Reiki or other types of healing because of its absorbent qualities. As this stone works with the root chakra, it's great to use when healing the nervous system, lower body parts, and reproductive system.

CELESTITE

Celestite, also called celestine, is a beautiful pale blue crystal that helps with understanding, meditation, and mindfulness. This crystal belongs to the orthorhombic **crystal system** (or a grouping according to symmetry), and it looks "raw" in appearance, with jutting shiny and smooth faces, resulting in a prismatic effect. Although it looks similar to quartz, the chemical makeup is different; it contains sulfate strontium rather than silicate and oxygen atoms. These crystals are naturally soft and shouldn't be placed in direct sunlight or in water.

This crystal is associated with the throat and higher chakras, as it has the ability to connect you to higher consciousness. This stone brings pure peace and clarity, as it is connected to celestial source energy. It is also connected to the zodiac sign of Taurus. Celestite facilitates perception and expression of higher energies. If you are working with any mental issues, this crystal can help you to release what is keeping you held in polarity. It's also a particularly great stone to work with when you are feeling balanced and wish to take your meditations to the next level, as it can help you reach transcendental states.

JADE

Jade is a vivid green stone that brings good luck, clarity, wisdom, and heart awareness. Most often, it's found in its common form, called jadeite or nephrite jade, which is readily found in the United States. Jade can also be quite expensive, because 70 percent of the world's jade supply comes from Myanmar and it's difficult to mine. Jade will often be found in its polished, hand-held form, but comes in all shapes and sizes.

Jade is associated with the heart chakra and the grounded and loving sign of Taurus. It connects you to the wisdom of the planet. This crystal can help in fertility matters and childbirth. Natural green jade is harmonizing to the whole body and nourishes your nervous system by helping you to release negative thoughts. This stone brings about balance and encourages moderation. It's also a protective stone, promoting self-sufficiency and bringing about safety. You can use jade in dreamwork as well, as this facilitates lucid dreaming and remembering your dreams. This stimulating yet mellow crystal is more of a rare find, but an excellent choice to add to your collection if you are looking for high-vibrational, heart-centered healing.

LEMURIAN QUARTZ

Lemurian quartz, also known as Lemurian seed quartz, is a member of the quartz family. It has a raw and somewhat cloudy appearance. Lemurian quartz is clear or dusted with pink (from hematite), and has many striations on the surface. They can be found with "keys" or notches that indicate the crystal may have been used in the past to program information. This special crystal can be found in parts of Brazil, Hawaii, and in the Arkansas crystal vein in the United States. Connecting to these crystals will help you to awaken hidden gifts and connect you more fully to your multidimensional self through your crown and heart chakras.

Legend has it that Lemurian quartz went underground when the civilization disappeared from the face of the Earth, and by holding these crystals today, you are able to unlock years of precious energy codes (information) that have been stored in the gems themselves. They carry a message of unity consciousness and oneness and some believe they contain the secrets to humanity's greatest healing.

Lemurian quartz is associated with the zodiac sign of Gemini. It is often used in gridwork, as quartz is a strong amplifier and will raise the vibration of all the crystals around it.

FLUORITE

Fluorite, composed of calcium fluoride, belongs to a crystal family called halide minerals. This stone crystallizes in an isometric cubic pattern and can often be found raw or polished, in towers and various cuts. Fluorite is found all over the world. Relatively easy to find for purchase, this crystal is affordable. Ranging in shades from bluish-green to deep purple banding, fluorite often has bands of all types of blues, greens, and purples within the same stone. This translucent crystal looks stunning catching the Sun's rays, but be careful not to get it wet, because water can damage it.

Fluorite is best known for its mental enhancing properties, bringing focus and clarity. It's associated with the third eye chakra and corresponds to the zodiac sign of Gemini. Fluorite will allow thoughts to untangle within the mind. It's a helpful choice for students, writers, and anyone else who needs to stay focused. This crystal is thought to boost the immune system, strengthen bones, and boost inflammation response. It's also said to help clear the aura.

BLUE SODALITE

Blue sodalite, a tectosilicate mineral, supports communication, positive thoughts, authenticity, and awareness. This member of the feldspathoid crystal family contains sodium and is not a silicate. It can be confused with lapis lazuli due to its deep blue, opaque appearance. Sodalite is an affordable stone that contains veins of white throughout and may be polished or unpolished. Originally found in Greenland, most sodalite today comes from the United States, Canada, and parts of Russia.

Sodalite is a choice stone for working with the throat chakra and is associated with the zodiac sign of Gemini. This crystal encourages rational thoughts and organization. It assists with focus, clarity, and expression through verbalization. This stone can also aid in understanding your spiritual direction and recalibration if you are offtrack. If you are having trouble with your thyroid, metabolism, or vocal cords, or you are experiencing calcium deficiency, blue sodalite can help. Great for speaking your highest truth, blue sodalite encourages you to stay on mission and speak out.

CHRYSOCOLLA

Chrysocolla is an incredible heart healing stone that soothes the emotional body with a cool, calming energy. This opaque crystal is similar to turquoise in appearance. It is cyan-blue with vivid green splotches and marbling. Chrysocolla can be found in Africa, Israel, Peru, Mexico, and the southwestern United States. This copper-rich mineral is in the orthorhombic crystal system, and is sometimes infused with malachite, turquoise, quartz, or azurite. It is usually sold in small or medium polished pieces and is relatively affordable and easy to find. Don't leave this one in the open too long, as the Sun's rays can scorch and fade the vibrant colors.

Chrysocolla is associated with the root, throat, and heart chakras and the zodiac sign of Cancer. This is a strengthening and balancing stone, calling in serenity and grace. This is an extremely grounding crystal, keeping you protected, present, and calm. It helps with finding the courage to forgive and can ease feelings of loneliness. Chrysocolla encourages self-awareness and is said to help aid in lowering blood pressure. As a heart opener, this crystal can help you to access the love inside, amplify it, and radiate it out to others.

LARIMAR

Larimar, the stone of the ocean, is especially rare, as its only known source is from a mountainous province in the Dominican Republic. Drawing its name from the Spanish word for sea, "mar," this sky-blue, opaque crystal undergoes a unique cooling process during crystallization that gives it a marbled effect. This crystal is a rare variety of the acid silicate mineral pectolite that forms in the cavities within basaltic lava. It is only found in smaller pieces and can be quite expensive.

Larimar is associated with the throat and sacral chakras and the zodiac sign of Cancer. This crystal is extremely tranquil and soothing. The seafoam-blue stone purifies the entire auric body, welcomes grace and ease, promotes authentic expression, and harmonizes the body and soul.

PEACH MOONSTONE

Peach moonstone is a warm and cheerful stone, inviting balance and receptiveness to blessings headed your way. Peach moonstone is a semitranslucent stone that varies in shades from peachy-pink to light brownish-tan. It has a multidimensional, shimmering quality because of its mineral base of potassium aluminum silicate feldspar. With a somewhat milky tinge, the peach moonstone is commonly found polished in all shapes and sizes, with palm-sized stones being moderate to affordable in cost.

Peach moonstone is associated with the sacral and solar plexus chakras and the zodiac sign of Cancer. This is a lucky crystal representing new beginnings. It helps reconnect you to your passions, creativity, and joy. Due to its connection to the sacral chakra, it also helps stimulate the reproductive center and invokes parental energies. Peach moonstone harmonizes hormonal imbalances, calms emotions, and fosters openness to change. When you need to let things go and aren't sure where to begin, call on peach moonstone. The stone of playfulness and flow will also help you embrace each moment for what it is, reminding you that you do not need to change anything to find your true happiness.

CITRINE

Citrine, the sunny stone of positivity, is a member of the quartz family. Typically found in hues of yellow-orange, this translucent crystal gets its coloration from the traces of iron oxide found in it. After amethyst, it's the most popular quartz type. In fact, these two crystals often appear together because of their molecular similarities. Citrines are commonly found in Brazil, Uruguay, and Russia, and you can find them polished for purchase in small or large pieces. Citrine is also popularly sold in its raw form, as this crystal forms lovely prismatic faces.

Citrine is associated with the solar plexus chakra and the zodiac sign of Leo. This stone increases your optimism and joy. It helps you connect to your purpose, encourages sharing, and brings out your courageous side. Often, you'll see this stone used in manifestation rituals for its ability to bring abundance and attune you with the energy of prosperity. Citrine is a self-esteem booster that can ease self-doubt and worries. You can't help but smile when you have this stone around.

SUNSTONE

The stone of luck and blessings, sunstone is a bright and optimistic crystal of the feldspar group. It belongs to the plagioclase family and sometimes goes by the name "heliolite." This semitranslucent orange-red stone contains golden tones and flecks of hematite or copper that give it a glittery appearance. Some rare pieces contain a rainbow lattice, or striations of rainbow-colored flecks, called rainbow lattice sunstone, though the most commonly found type is orange, white, and sparkly. Found in India, Tanzania, and Oregon in the United States, this mineral is abundant and easily found in small palm-sized polished stone pieces. This one loves to be charged out in the Sun.

Sunstone is associated with the solar plexus and sacral chakras and the zodiac sign of Leo. This crystal is not only stunning in appearance but can also be used to treat a variety of conditions. It is thought to hold the energy of the Sun and transmit the light energy to anywhere in the body it is needed, lifting the lower vibrations and bringing healing. Sunstone helps manage stress levels and assists in carving out healthy boundaries. It encourages independence, originality, and creativity.

AMAZONITE

Amazonite is one of the strongest heart-amplifying crystals, and among the most captivating. This brilliant green-blue stone, also known as Amazon jade, is a tectosilicate containing a potassium feldspar called microcline. This opaque crystal is easy to shape into beads, so you'll see it used often in jewelry or lapidary work. The colors in this stone can range from pale to vivid green, with a high saturation, occasionally interrupted by streaks of white feldspar. It also has a glimmering sheen that floats below the surface, giving this crystal a mystical, multi-dimensional look. Amazonite has been found worldwide.

Amazonite is associated with the heart chakra and the zodiac sign of Leo. A powerful energy booster, amazonite keeps the doors of the heart open so that love can flow freely and be received and magnified. It encourages your nervous system to recalibrate after trauma and opens you to releasing anger. You can also use this stone to welcome in forgiveness as you step into a clean energy slate. Use amazonite to help you heal after illness and when you want to get a peaceful night's rest, as well.

ROSE QUARTZ

The ultimate stone of love, rose quartz is a high vibrational member of the quartz family. It gets its name from its baby-pink, rosy coloration. The translucent crystal is a coarse-grained variety of the silica mineral quartz, found in pegmatite rocks. Shades of rose quartz may vary from delicate pale to rich dark pink. Rose quartz, like clear quartz, is found in abundance all over the world. It is mostly found in huge slabs, so you'll often see this rock both polished and raw, in many shapes and sizes. Direct sunlight may fade the vibrancy of your rose quartz, so don't let this one stay in the Sun for too long.

Rose quartz is associated with the heart chakra and the zodiac sign of Virgo. This soft and gentle crystal is a reminder of the unconditional love we hold inside. We are always able to access this love, even when it is buried under a hard shell. Rose quartz lovingly helps you have patience as you tend to your emotional wounds and reminds you that you always have a choice to be kind. This crystal opens you up to greater connection with your higher self.

LEPIDOLITE

Stunning purple-pink and pearly, lepidolite is a unique lithium-rich mineral that assists in clearing anxiety from the system. This lilac crystal is supersoft and flaky, requiring delicate care. It forms in a pseudohexagonal lattice system and can be found in thin, scaly slabs, plates, or palm-stones. Flashy and metallic, lepidolite occurs mostly in granite pegmatites. It is found worldwide, most notably in Brazil, Australia, Mexico, Europe, Russia, and the United States. Because this crystal is especially soft, smudge-cleansing is recommended, as water could soften the specimen and run the risk of dissolving it entirely.

Lepidolite is associated with the third eye and crown chakras and the zodiac sign of Virgo. Due to the trace amounts of natural lithium found in this crystal, lepidolite is extremely good for emotional balancing, meditation, and tension relief. It also helps clear electromagnetic pollutants from the environment, which makes it great to keep near laptops, charging areas, and Wi-Fi stations. Calming and relaxing, lepidolite is a great stone to put under your pillow or on a nightstand to help you with a restful sleep, as this crystal promotes tranquility and relieves insomnia.

APOPHYLLITE

Apophyllite is known as the stone of the angels, giving you access to your own higher self, as well as the angelic realms. Apophyllite is a semitranslucent white or colorless crystal, and many examples contain peach-colored inclusions on their many square-shaped, prismatic faces. Formed from ancient lava flows, this crystal is birthed inside geodes, or pockets inside the molten rock. The stone is often found and sold in raw hunks, in a variety of colors, wherever basalt and lava zones exist. The stone is flaky and soft, so use care not to get it wet.

Apophyllite is associated with the crown chakra and the zodiac sign of Virgo. This crystal can be used to open up spiritual channels and communicate with your angel team. It facilitates access to higher perspectives, and helps you integrate higher learning. Representing purity, peace, and unconditional love, apophyllite will raise your vibrations and dispel doubts and worries. This is an extremely soft crystal that helps you access gentleness and forgiveness. They make excellent room-chargers, raising the frequency and harmonic resonance of any space. Apophyllite assists in building your extrasensory abilities by gracefully expanding your consciousness.

RAINBOW MOONSTONE

Rainbow moonstone, the companion of labradorite, is a stone of balance and receptivity. Like the Moon, this milky-white stone represents receptivity, vulnerability, and internal strength. Rainbow moonstone is a semitranslucent stone that contains blue iridescent flecks that flash with a rainbow sheen across the surface of the stone. It's more commonly known for its adularescence, which gives the crystal its flashy sheen. As a yin-oriented crystal, this feminine stone loves to charge by the light of the full Moon.

Moonstone is associated with the sacral chakra and the zodiac sign of Libra. The stone of the Divine Mother, it represents new beginnings, birth, and divine intuition. Expect new blessings when working with this crystal, and be prepared to go within to find the next steps to your path. Moonstone helps nurture your emotions and comfort you through times of transformation. This crystal facilitates cleansing, as it tunes you into the element of water. It assists in boosting your intuition and psychic abilities, as well. Work with moonstone to illuminate new perspectives within the shadows of the unknown as you create the template for who you are becoming next in this lifetime.

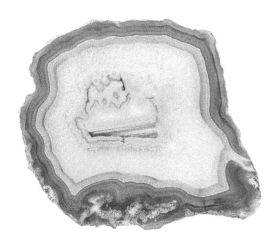

AGATE

Agate is a master healing stone, used to treat the entire energy field. This banded microcrystalline quartz contains lovely patterns and marbling, and comes in a variety of shades, including brownish-gray, sand, white, and black. Each stone comes with a unique pattern, giving each its own personality and vibration. They are commonly found on shores, beaches, and in gravel or sediment along the side of the road, making this stone easily accessible for those willing to hunt for it. Mines are located worldwide, but these crystals are especially abundant along the Pacific coast of the United States. Because of their popularity and prevalence, they make for excellent lapidary creations such as jewelry, cabochons, and beads.

Agate is associated with the all chakras as well as your aura, giving it the ability to clear and balance your entire energy field. It is linked with the zodiac sign of Libra. Agate is a gentle yet powerful ally, able to eliminate and transform negativity quickly. This stone facilitates concentration, mental focus, and analytical abilities. Agate also reinforces a sense of safety, providing a feel of grounded protection and support and making it a great choice for navigating life's difficulties.

SELENITE

Selenite, the crystallized form of gypsum, is a master cleansing crystal. Used to clean other crystals and for energy clearing in individuals, this stone is a powerhouse purification tool. This translucent and chalky calcium sulfate is one of the softest crystals included in this book, so it should stay away from water. Found on every continent, selenite is mined in huge slabs and sold as wands or bricks. It's easy to identify from its stark white appearance, with a mild luster and silky surface sheen. You'll likely be able to feel its instant calming effects.

Selenite is associated with the all chakras, but especially the crown chakra and above. You can use selenite to cut cords, remove blockages, and balance your chakra column, which includes all of your energy centers. With its natural ability to balance and clear energy, selenite is linked to the zodiac sign of Libra. Not only does this crystal elevate your spirit, but it helps eliminate attachments and dissolve impurities from your auric field, as well. Consider working with this stone similar to taking a refreshing light bath, as you use it to wash away uncomplimentary vibrations, welcoming in clarity and renewed energy.

GARNET

Garnet, a deep ruby red stone, is a semiprecious gemstone that is both a grounding stone and a crystal that ignites passion. Made of silicate, garnets form in cubes within a rhombic dodecahedron, a twelve-sided crystal containing diamond-shaped faces. This unique shape is only specific to garnets. Though they can form in many colors, are most often seen in their traditional dark red hues. These opaque stones may come polished or raw, and are often found in India, Myanmar, China, and Australia.

Garnet can connect you with your root chakra and is associated with the zodiac sign of Scorpio. It reconnects with your sexuality and can help spark passion. It's helpful to anchor in energies of stability if you feel out of control, and tune you back into self-love through deep awareness. This is a stone of confidence that can help to reawaken the heart, courage, and hope. This crystal is thought to help purify the blood as well, boosting and balancing energy levels. This is a powerful stone, so use it in select healings.

LABRADORITE

Labradorite is found in igneous rocks around the world but originally appeared in Canada. The color and sheen seem to change when held at varying angles, with hues ranging from blues and greens to yellows purples. Its companion stone is rainbow moonstone, which also presents with flashy specks across the stone's surface, but is much lighter in color (usually white). Often sold polished to increase their luster, labradorites are popular in beautiful lapidary pieces (such a jewelry), at an affordable price.

Labradorite is used for various chakra work, including the throat and third eye. It's associated with the sign of Scorpio because of its support in anchoring transformational energies. Used to facilitate personal growth, expand spiritual awareness, break old habits, and focus the mind, this stone is helpful when you are going through times of death/rebirth. Labradorite helps ease harsh energies of abrupt change and opens up creative channels instead so the new energy can be optimized and harnessed more readily. It's easy to align with a higher frequency with the help of labradorite.

OBSIDIAN

Obsidian, once a stone used in the rituals of ancient Egypt for its protective qualities, is one of the strongest grounding crystals ever to come from the Earth. Formed from an erupting volcano as the viscous lava flow cools, obsidian is technically igneous rock. This volcanic glass is shiny, dark black, and opaque, with a glossy sheen. It cannot be classified under any crystal or mineral system. It is collected in locations that have had volcanic activity in the past, including the northwestern United States, Canada, Chile, Greece, and Brazil.

Obsidian is perfect for healing the root chakra and is associated with the zodiac sign of Scorpio. A major detoxification stone, obsidian helps purify toxins of the mind, mental field, and any physical organs. In ancient rituals, priestesses would lay on giant slabs of obsidian to cleanse themselves of unwanted energies. Born through fire, it has emerged anew and helps you cross over through the death/rebirth portals of your life. When everything around you is changing, obsidian energy brings stability and anchors you to your highest reality. It offers you a different perspective and leads you to the decisions you are destined to choose.

PYRITE

Commonly known as "fool's gold," pyrite is the most abundant and widespread disulfide mineral crystal in the world. Part of the cubic crystal system, this metallic, opaque crystal forms in sparkly and shiny cubic stacks. It can be found in quartz veins, inside metamorphic rock, or in geothermal pockets. The "gold" cubes form faces with symmetrical, aesthetically pleasing sides, so this crystal is often sold in its raw form. Because oxidation of pyrite can release toxins and the sulfur content inside can create sulfuric acid when infused with water, do not get this one wet.

Pyrite is associated with the solar plexus and the zodiac sign of Sagittarius. It enhances your memory, increases optimism, and helps bring embodiment awareness. Often considered good luck, pyrite is a symbol of material abundance. This stone also acts as a grounding stone, protecting against negativity on physical, emotional, and etheric levels. Pyrite loves to be paired with other grounding stones, such as obsidian, onyx, and tourmaline, or stones for the crown chakra, such as clear quartz. Put them in a grid or together on an altar to maximize their energetic effects.

SERPENTINE

Serpentine gets its name from its snakelike appearance and coloration and its usefulness in working with kundalini energy. Found in a number of shades of green, serpentine is a magnesium silicate found in flat, tabular, crystal shapes or waxy shards. Often sold in its raw form, serpentine can be found worldwide. Associated with the sacral and crown chakras, this stone corresponds with the sign of Scorpio.

Kundalini is shakti energy, which rises up your spine; it is intense as well as sensual, helping to connect you with your inner god or goddess. Serpentine helps facilitate the rising of your personal kundalini, helping to clear each chakra as you go. This stone is excellent for remembering and integrating your past lives. It also helps correct mental and emotional imbalances and opens up a pathway to the crown chakra, which it stimulates. Detoxifying for the body and blood, this stone is extremely cleansing and powerful.

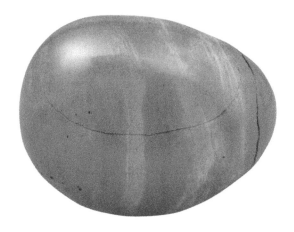

RED JASPER

Red jasper, an earth-energy crystal, is a grounding stone that sometimes acts like a fire stone, inspiring passion and purpose. This root chakra crystal corresponds to the sign of Sagittarius and displays as a deep, fire-red color due to the iron oxide in its mineral base. Used by Native Americans, as well as ancient Middle Eastern cultures, this stone has traditionally adorned pottery and been used for healing purposes. Large mineral veins of jasper can be found in South America, Australia, and Western Europe. Like the carnelian, this opaque chalcedony stone displays no lattice to the naked eye and appears smooth and uniform on the surface. There may be mineral bands running through it. You'll find this stone for purchase as a polished piece in various shades, shapes, and sizes.

Jasper's healing properties include blood tonifying and pressure relief, overall balancing, and increasing strength. As an earth element stone, it can help to stabilize energies and increase self-trust, as well as eliminate distortion and distractions. Serving as a stone of protection, this lush stone feels nurturing and comforting, and is excellent in healing inner-child trauma or learning to repattern and re-parent yourself.

TOURMALINE

Tourmaline is a potent and powerful ally for cleansing negative energies, grounding, and protection. This boron silicate mineral is formed in slabs that look like shards, both big and small. Tourmaline is predominantly mined from Brazil, Africa, and California. It is known to come in a few shades: pink, green, and opaque black. Watermelon tourmaline is translucent and has both pink and green. The different colors hold the same properties vibrationally, yet perform different jobs. For example, black tourmaline is excellent for the root chakra, while pink, green and watermelon tourmaline work best on the heart space.

Associated with the sign of Capricorn, tourmaline reflects the heavy energy of the earth element, helping to stabilize energies. Watermelon tourmaline promotes feelings of self-worth and confidence. Black tourmaline is an excellent immune and nervous system aid, as well as a detoxifying crystal. This stone helps rid you of negativity and uncomplimentary energies. Like a black hole, it swallows up toxic vibrations, leaving you purified and sparkling clean. It can be very strong in its abilities to heal and remove blockages, so use your best judgment when using this stone.

MALACHITE

Malachite is a powerful stone of self-love and breaking bad habits. This crystal belongs to the monoclinic crystal system, and has an opaque, deep green appearance with lighter green bands and marbling. Often sold as polished gems, this is a semiprecious stone and can be on the pricier side for small- to medium-sized pieces. It's on the softer end, so keep it out of water. Most malachite is found in Africa, Mexico, Australia, and Russia.

Malachite is traditionally a stone for the heart chakra, although it's so powerful that you can also use it to ground yourself or for any root chakra work. It's associated with the zodiac sign of Capricorn, and matches this sign in its earthy, bold, and rich energy. This is a great crystal to work with when dealing with mental disturbances, toxic emotions, and old behavior patterns that are no longer working for you. This stone helps you tune into unconditional love, especially self-love. It can reveal and heal old wounds, and clear the way for you to move forward with forgiveness. Malachite is a well-known protection stone and can also help to guard against radiation and pollutants from the atmosphere.

CLEAR QUARTZ

Clear quartz is the world's most well-known and commonly found crystal. This mineral is rich in silicon dioxide and is found in all of the major crystal beds. Quartz has a hexagonal crystalline structure and comes in almost any shade, size, cut, and price. Clear quartz is transparent but may have inclusions on the inside, which are tiny bits of other minerals that are trapped inside the crystal during its formation. When selecting a clear quartz, purity and clarity are strictly a matter of preference. Rutilated clear quartz, for example, contains striated mineral deposits that are aesthetically pleasing and give the crystal a different energetic feel. You may bathe your clear quartz in sunlight, moonlight, or water.

Clear quartz is associated with the crown chakra and the sign of Capricorn in the zodiac. It can absorb energy, light, and information, as well as store it within its crystalline structure. This crystal is an excellent energy amplifier and regulator, so it's ideal for working with in grids and on altar spaces, with your other crystals. Quartz helps you connect with wisdom and your higher self. It can also revitalize your physical, emotional, and spiritual planes with ease and grace.

AMETHYST

Amethyst is a powerful third eye opener and psychic protection stone. This crystal is a variety of quartz, with a traditional hexagonal structure. Unlike its cousin clear quartz, this silicon dioxide stone often has a purple coloration from its irradiation or iron inclusions. Occasionally, you may also find amethyst in pinkish purple or light green hues, though it's rare. It's prevalent all over the world, and large deposits can be found in Brazil, Uruguay, Mexico, France, Australia, and Africa. This crystal loves to play with other stones, but don't leave it outside too long, as it may fade with prolonged exposure to the Sun.

Amethyst is associated with the third eye chakra and the zodiac sign of Aquarius. A calming stone, it promotes relaxation and balances the mind. As you work with this stone, your third eye may become more sensitive. You will gain a level of spiritual awareness and your intuitive abilities will increase. It's common to start to "see" behind the veil of illusions, cutting through obstacles in your way and directing you to the highest possible outcome. This stone is also known as the sobriety stone, helping you to get clear and maintain a clear auric field.

TURQUOISE

Turquoise helps bring beauty, balance, and inner calm. This crystal is a hydrated copper and aluminum phosphate mineral, often found in basalt sandstone in arid environments such as the southwestern United States, Mexico, Chile, China, and Tibet. This stunning opaque crystal ranges from light blue to vivid greenish-blue, with veins of matrix (the surrounding rock sediment) infused throughout. This stone is less common to find and is considered a semiprecious gem. You'll normally see this as small, polished pieces.

Turquoise is associated with the throat and third eye chakras, and the zodiac sign of Aquarius. Used to gain balance, wisdom, and strength, this is an intensely powerful stone for healing. Turquoise dispels negative energies and protects you against depression and exhaustion. It assists in creative problem-solving and helps clarify new directions and ideas. This crystal is said to enhance the immune system as well as the body's absorption of minerals. It additionally purifies the respiratory system, brings down inflammation, and cleans out acidic anxiety from the body.

AQUAMARINE

Aquamarine, or "water of the sea," is a translucent, pale blue semiprecious gemstone that calms and reduces stress. This translucent crystal is naturally very light to blue to blue-green, and has excellent clarity, which invokes the peace of crystal blue waters. Mined mainly in Brazil, Madagascar, Australia, and Pakistan, this variety of mineral is called beryl. It mostly forms in mineral-rich pegmatite rocks (a type of igneous rock). Crystals tend to be hexagonal, with a flat top or pointed as a prism. Raw aquamarine can be very large due to the crystal structure, but most of the pieces mined and sold are a few inches in length.

Aquamarine is associated with the throat and third eye chakras and the zodiac sign of Aquarius. Though this crystal is connected to the water element, it is also perfect for air signs, as it aids in connecting with the breath, lungs, and throat. This crystal is perfect for sensitive souls because of its incredibly gentle energy. It's calming like cool waters and helps release as water does by cleansing your aura. Aquamarine is a master purification stone and can be used like selenite to cut energetic cords or clear blockages. It also has a shielding effect on your energy field, helping to protect against unwanted energies.

LAPIS LAZULI

Lapis lazuli, or lapis, is an extremely psychic stone, often used to enhance intuition. This favorite of ancient Egypt is an opaque semiprecious stone normally found in shades of vivid royal blue to midnight blue, with splotches of gold pyrite and white calcite. This metamorphic rock gets its sapphire-like coloration from lazulite (a blue silicate mineral) and can often be found in limestone. Most of the lapis sold today is mined primarily from Afghanistan, Chile, Siberia, Myanmar, and parts of the United States. In ancient days, it was used in jewelry, decor, and pottery in the Indus Valley, Mesopotamia, and Egypt.

Lapis lazuli is associated with the throat and third eye chakras and the zodiac sign of Pisces. This highly spiritual stone is said to be the crystal of friendship and truth. It will help to facilitate the expression of your highest truth, and create ease in the relationships in your life. As a third eye opener, this stone allows you to access your innate psychic abilities effortlessly. It can also bring protection from psychic attacks.

HOWLITE

Howlite, also known as white turquoise, is said to assist with memory and keep you calm. This opaque calcium borosilicate mineral has a monoclinic structure and looks chalky white with gray marbling. Most howlite comes from Los Angeles, California, but deposits have also been found in other parts of the world, like Turkey, Mexico, Europe, and Russia. You'll find pieces of howlite both large and small, polished, and affordably priced, as this is not a semiprecious stone like its sister turquoise. These crystals love to be parts of grids with different types of quartz.

Howlite is associated with the third eye chakra and the zodiac sign of Pisces. It represents patience and perspective, and is an excellent stone for past-life regression work. This stone is also a good choice for studying or writing, as it brings awareness and focus. It is said to balance the calcium levels in the body and strengthen hair, bones, teeth, and muscles. Howlite is a supportive stone for integrating your life's lessons and memories in a nurturing way.

BLACK KYANITE

Black kyanite is a powerful stone that grounds and energizes simultaneously. This crystal is less commonly than its sister stone, blue kyanite, but even more energetically potent. Black kyanite is an opaque crystal that appears in flat, fanlike blade formations. Pieces of kyanite are often found in large slabs, which can flake off into smaller pieces. They are relatively soft and shouldn't be placed in water. Aluminum-rich, this silicate mineral forms in pegmatite rock at extremely high pressure (this is why it's useful when you are facing high-pressure situations). These crystals are often found in Brazil, though large deposits exist in Burma, India, and Africa, too.

Black kyanite is associated with the root and throat chakras and the zodiac sign of Pisces. It is known as the "Great Awakener," as it clears and shields your energy. Great for dispelling negativity and uprooting worries in the subconscious mind, this stone is the ultimate crystal for deep inner work. When you are feeling drained, use black kyanite to restore your energy reserves and bring you back to center. As a member of the kyanite family, this variety will help to facilitate your highest level of expression.

PART III

CRYSTAL PRACTICES FOR SUN, MOON & RISING SIGNS

The next part of this book will cover practices for your Sun, Moon, and ascending or rising signs. Remember that the big three represent your identity, internal self, and how you appear to others. Though these are main elements of your birth chart, you'll also want to pay attention to the ruling planet within each, as the planetary placements have influence on the sign itself, as well as your energy. In this next chapter, you are going to connect your love of crystals with astrology, learning some simple mindfulness techniques. We will explore simple, coherent, and impactful wellness exercises.

The insights gained from these practices will highlight strengths, potentials, and challenges, creating awareness of different areas of your life. You'll be better equipped to manage your own behaviors and relationships and any opportunities that lay ahead. Understanding how your Sun, Moon, and rising signs work within you will allow you to operate as your best self.

CHAPTER 5

CRYSTAL PRACTICES FOR SUN SIGNS

A s the Sun radiates, it beams energy across the solar system. Its energy is essential, therefore the Sun is a prominent part of your birth chart. It represents your sense of self, ego, core identity, and purpose. Everything you are motivated to do and become stems from your Sun sign, as this sign is the foundational element fueling your being. For some, discovering their life's true meaning and reason for being takes a lifetime. By using astrology as a consciousness map, you can harness your unique potential and optimize your life according to what truly drives you. When your purpose and actions match, you are in alignment. Alignment not only feels the best for your body, mind, and spirit, but helps you focus and enhances every part of your life.

You probably already understand many of the things that make you feel the best (as well as things that don't). These things highlight your personality and form your identity, which you broadcast into the world. The practices in the next chapter are aimed at bringing you joy and allowing you to experience life at its fullest, from your happy place.

ARIES SUN: MIRROR DANCING

Connect to your inner fire through this surrendered movement, dance-inspired ritual. This practice will help you become more aware and embodied inside your own body. Aries is highly action-oriented, so the ignition switch is always on. It's often difficult for you to slow down, being the supercharged leader that you are. You tend to be highly aware and confident and don't mind showing that side off. This is your chance to embrace it, taking the time to bring awareness to your embodiment and connecting to your fire element.

✦ **Crystal: carnelian**

✦ **A playlist that includes slow songs, varying in tempo and length. The songs should be downtempo while inspiring movement.**

✦ **A mirror positioned so you can see yourself.**

Use this exercise privately to reach the places inside that don't get attention while you are on the go.

1. Place your carnelian in the room in which you are practicing. Make sure you are positioned near a reflective surface or mirror. Turn on your music.

2. Feel into the moment with presence. Start to move your body, even if you simply sway gently in place for a while; anything goes, as long as you are moving.

3. Observe yourself, then let go and allow the dance to take over. If you feel stuck, grab your carnelian and hold it with you while you embrace however you are showing up.

4. Try to get through a few songs, and rest afterward to observe what kind of feelings came up for you during your movement therapy.

TAURUS SUN: FOUR CORNERS WALKING MEDITATION

This practice will help you center your energies, particularly in areas where you may feel depleted. Taurus Sun energy is all about building healthy and strong foundations. Success for you requires reflection and presence.

✦ **Crystal: smoky quartz**

You will be walking the four corners of the room in which you spend the most time. You will reflect on the energies present for you and call in new energies to fill your spiritual tank. This exercise follows a traditional Native American medicine wheel.

1. Hold your smoky quartz and start in the east corner of your room.

2. Ruminate here on your inner vision and spend some time figuring out where you stand in this moment.

3. Move to the south corner, representing the physical aspects and timing of your life. Relate to what is currently on your mind from a different angle.

4. Move to the west corner. Use the gift of reason to sort your vision and figure out what roles the characters play, and what meaning you are assigning to the stories around your vision.

5. Walk to the north corner, representing the mental realms of culture and language.

6. Ask for grounding, and then place the stone down in that corner when you feel complete.

7. You may retrieve the stone at a later time after the four-corners walk is complete or when you feel it is right to do so.

GEMINI SUN: HIGHEST-SELF MEDITATION

Gemini Sun is oriented toward matters of the mind, and as such, you can become distracted easily, allowing your worries to overcome you. The following meditation and crystal work can help you to calm your thoughts as you embrace and focus your mental energies. Connecting to the part of you that seeks to explore various speeds, mindsets, and avenues all day will help you to become more embodied and trust the direction in which life is taking you.

✦ **Crystal: Lemurian quartz**

✦ **A quiet and private space where you can meditate undisturbed for 20 to 30 minutes.**

As a Gemini Sun, you have a tendency to go a million directions at once, which can leave anyone feeling overwhelmed. It's time to embrace your multidimensionality and tune into your highest self. Let go and trust the process.

1. Hold your Lemurian quartz or place it in your palm while you sit. Say aloud to yourself, "Allow me to connect now with my highest self. Let all that is needed be known. Help me to experience the version(s) of reality that best serves my soul."

2. Begin by breathing slowly in and out for a minute or two, following your inhalations and exhalations with your awareness.

3. You may have a question, or something you are sorting out. Feel free to ask your higher self. Let your higher self guide you.

4. Lie down and place the crystal on your forehead. Continue to receive any information, feelings, visuals, colors, or other inputs you are able to perceive.

5. End the meditation when you feel complete or information has stopped coming in.

CANCER SUN: HOME SWEET HOME

A Cancer Sun's greatest sanctuary is their home. Feeling safe and sound is what nourishes you. As a creature of comfort, you are concerned with physical surroundings and can tend to need a place to process your intense emotions, away from others. This practice will help you to cultivate a serene and secure home environment by using plant medicine and crystal energy to protect your personal space.

+ **Crystal: chrysocolla**

+ **Matches**

+ **Some dried bundled aromatic plant material**

+ **Ashtray or a plate to catch embers**

In this practice, you'll be harnessing the protective qualities of chrysocolla and smudging the spaces you spend the most time in. Smudging is an ancient practice of clearing the air by ritual burning.

1. You will be blessing your crystals and space and setting the energetics of your room to keep out any negativities. Begin by lighting the smudge stick and using the smoke to clear the corners of the room, as well as the doorways. Wave the smudge into the places your intuition is telling you need clearing, and let the smoke waft up.

2. Think about what you are getting "rid" of energetically as you smudge. Open the windows, if possible.

3. Smudge your crystal(s).

4. Place your chrysocolla on the window sill or under your pillow to secure your space against any uncomplimentary energy and banish any feelings of sadness or loneliness.

LEO SUN: ABUNDANCE ALL DAY

As a Leo Sun, you are a natural attractor, your energy magnetizes people, things, and situations to you effortlessly. This practice will help you bring awareness to the things that are truly meant for you. Remember, just because it comes to you doesn't mean it's for your highest good. At the same time, you won't be denied the things you desire, as you bring together your personal fire energy with a bright and powerful citrine crystal. Citrine is here to remind you that you *can* have it all, if you focus your intention.

✦ **Crystal: citrine**

By carrying a citrine stone with you, you'll not only help to attract prosperity, but you will also open the channels of abundance to flow in and around you, in all areas of life. This crystal promotes positivity and banishes self-doubt, bringing you confidence and joy.

1. Think of something you are hoping to manifest. Keep it simple when first starting out. It could be patience, harmony, love, or financial abundance.

2. Carry your citrine with you or keep it close to your work space as a reminder of your intention. Every so often, pull it out, and think about what you are creating. Spend a moment or two in the energy of what it feels like to already have or be with that thing.

3. Repeat this whenever necessary or when working on a new manifestation.

VIRGO SUN: WATER CLEANSING RITUAL

Connect to your sensual side as you treat yourself to a luxurious bath-time ritual. As a Virgo Sun, you are deeply nurturing and have a pattern of tending to the myriad of people and things pulling on your attention. This practice will help you ignite or enhance your devotion to yourself. After all, this is one relationship that can fall to the wayside all too easily.

+ **Crystal: rose quartz**

+ **Bathtub or foot tub**

+ **Rose petals and essential oils (try geranium, ylang-ylang and jasmine)**

This practice is centered around the rose quartz, which carries the energy of the divine feminine. This energy is caring, gentle, and radiantly beautiful. It knows when to let go and receive nourishment. You'll be taking the most luxurious bath, so get ready to relax and enjoy!

1. Put on some meditation music or soft sounds, and light some candles if you have them. Take time to set the mood.

2. Put a few drops of essential oils into your bath or foot tub, and top with a few select flower petals (roses work nicely).

3. Soak for 10 to 30 minutes. As you are soaking, place your rose quartz over top of your heart and say aloud, "I am love. I am loved. Allow me to open to the unconditional love that nourishes my soul. And so it is."

4. Bonus: Anoint yourself with the oil or fragrance of your choice after your bath for an enhanced experience.

5. Enjoy weekly or monthly for optimal benefits.

LIBRA SUN: BALANCING MOONSTONE MEDITATION

Always seeking balance as a Libra Sun, you manage a delicate dance between your friends, work, family, and personal life. Sometimes this is effortless, but other times, it can mean personal time is sacrificed. This meditation ritual is meant to help you get clear on any imbalances and help you arrive at a resolution to make your Libra heart sing with harmony.

+ **Crystals:
2 moonstones**

+ **Several pieces
of paper and
a pen**

This practice is centered around the moonstone crystal, which carries the energy of balance and new beginnings. This energy is nurturing, and opens you up to receive healing. This ritual is all about finding peace where you are, and welcoming in new energies to help you on the next step in your path. If you are at a crossroads, this can help you to discover a new direction.

1. Take your two pieces of paper to a quiet place where you can sit undisturbed.

2. Write down on each piece something that you wish to bring into balance in your life, such as work and personal life balance, financial freedom and travel, or time spent with a partner versus friends.

3. Place each piece under a separate moonstone crystal. It works nicely to have two crystals, but if you only have one, you can place them both pieces of paper under one crystal.

4. Say aloud, "I now call in balance in these areas of my life. May the solution find me, and help me find a way to devote more energy to the areas that need it most. And so it is!"

5. Leave the pieces of paper there for the next week, or until you start to notice your consciousness correcting the needed areas to align with your intention.

SCORPIO SUN: KUNDALINI AWAKENING

Scorpio Sun, your mystique is in being able to play and dance to a refined element of intimacy within. The song of kundalini awakening within your bones signals mastery over your personal energy. Known as the "coiled serpent," kundalini sits at the base of your spine until it is ready to make the ascent up your spinal column, moving through your chakras and cleansing your energy centers along the way. By working with this energy through the breath, you'll tap in to your watery depths and reawaken your sensual spirit, as well as relieve stress.

✦ **Crystal: serpentine**

✦ **Timer**

This practice incorporates serpentine, a stone that can help to heal issues related to the sacral chakra and reconnect you to your sensual energy. You will be using breath control and feeling into your own energy for this practice, so give yourself time to be able to notice an energetic shift. Repeat for three sets as often as needed.

1. Place your serpentine crystal next to you, and sit in cross-legged position.

2. Raise your arms above your head, fingers curled in and thumbs out, facing upward toward the sky.

3. Passively inhale, and actively exhale, in quick, sharp breaths. It will feel as though you are rapidly breathing into your diaphragm and forcibly releasing the breath.

4. Start with 30 seconds of this breathing, and when you are done, slowly lower your hands down with the last exhalation.

5. Pick up your stone and connect to it. Observe how your body and mind feel. Does your spinal channel feel clear?

6. Try to pull the energy up to your navel and allow your focus to remain there for a few moments.

SAGITTARIUS SUN: SOLAR-CHARGED ABUNDANCE

Just like the radiant Sun, you love to shine, Sagittarius Sun! This practice will help you to focus that sparkling energy on calling in abundance in all forms. Here, you are going to use the Sun element to connect to your highest expression in this lifetime!

✦ Crystal: pyrite

This practice is centered around pyrite, which is not only a grounding stone but also a stone of abundance. Pyrite is perfect for helping you tap into your infinite creator self and really sings beautifully alongside your fiery nature. For this exercise, you'll need to wait for a sunny day to work with your stone outside.

1. Take your pyrite to a spot in nature where it can get some sunlight.

2. Either lie down in savasana (yoga resting pose) or sit cross-legged.

3. Place the pyrite on your solar plexus or in your palm, whichever feels best.

4. Soak up the Sun's goodness for 10 to 20 minutes. Say aloud, "I have everything I need, especially _____. And so it is."

5. Take several breaths into your root (pelvic) chakra, belly, and heart space. Let the sunlight wash over you. If you want, leave your pyrite in the Sun for a few more hours to solar-charge.

6. Enjoy weekly or monthly for optimal benefits.

CAPRICORN SUN: EARTH WALK & CHARGE

Sensible and grounded, you are the person who your friends and coworkers go to for practical advice. Though, when you need advice, who do you go to for help? This practice will help establish your sovereignty as you work with tourmaline to make important decisions and direct your focus.

✦ **Crystal: tourmaline**

This practice is centered around the tourmaline crystal, which is a stone meant to deepen your connection to Earth. Use this exercise to ground and center yourself and your focus. Get ready to head outside to program your crystal. Enjoy monthly for optimal benefits.

1. Take your tourmaline out on a walk to a place you feel connected to the greenery.

2. Pause each time you see an inviting spot, staying for a few minutes and setting your crystal on its base (this works especially well with trees).

3. Let the energy of nature exchange vibrations with your crystal. As you do this, close your eyes and breathe deeply into your heart and then your root chakra (pelvic floor). As your crystal is charging, say aloud, "I receive grounding and clarity around _____. And so it is."

4. Pick something relevant and pertinent to whatever you are intending to focus on.

5. Commit to making one change that will take you in the direction you are being pointed toward whatever you've received some clarity about.

6. Pick up your crystal and move onto the next spot, and repeat these steps for the rest of your stroll.

AQUARIUS SUN: VISION-QUEST RITUAL

You are no stranger to tapping into your psychic senses, Aquarian Sun. This is your time to open your third eye and start manifesting. This practice will help you harness your imagination and intuition to create the life of your dreams. If you are brave enough to dream it, you deserve to bring it into reality.

✦ **Crystal: amethyst**

✦ **Magazine**

This practice is centered around the amethyst crystal, which is a potent stone for third eye expansion and accessing higher realms. Amethyst is perfect for helping you tap into your infinite potential. For this exercise, you'll want an old magazine you can cut up, and some alone time with your crystal.

1. Place your crystal on your third eye or in your palm. Breathe deeply and allow your mind to clear.

2. Say aloud, "I now open my third eye. Allow me to receive what I need to know about my future and the tools I need to reach my highest expression."

3. Allow any information that is needed to be received during your transmission. This includes any feelings, thoughts, visuals, colors, or words you perceive.

4. Take several breaths into your third eye. Open your eyes when you stop receiving information.

5. Take a look through your magazine once you've finished your meditation to select an image or word that best describes what you felt or saw during while in meditation. Cut it out, and place your crystal on top of it.

6. Leave your vision there until it comes into your current reality, or feel free to refresh it when needed.

PISCES SUN: DREAMWORK RITUAL

Pisces Sun, you thrive in delicate, ephemeral spaces that feel nurturing, dreamy, and supportive of your psychic acuity. This exercise is meant to aid you in your dream recall so you can access more of your psychic awareness, which exists both in the conscious and sub-conscious mind. You'll be setting your intentions before bed and then allowing your lapis crystal to aid in your dreamtime connection.

✦ **Crystal: lapis lazuli**

✦ **Dream journal or some paper to write on**

This practice is centered around the lapis lazuli crystal, which is a stone of intuition and aware-ness. This energy aids in opening the higher chakras to help you remember your dreams and clear subconscious blocks, as well as connecting your subconscious and conscious mind to boost your intuition and recall more of your life's purpose.

1. This exercise will be done from your bed, so come cozy and ready for sleep. Take your lapis to sleep with you, and place it under your pillow before bedtime.

2. Say aloud, "Help me to remember my dreams, and direct me to dreams that will best benefit my _____. And so it is!"

3. Go to sleep. As soon as you wake up, jot down what you remember from your dreams right away. Keep doing this daily until your dream recall improves.

4. Practice using your intuition to decode some of the symbolism and messages you may receive.

5. Perform daily for a few weeks at a time for optimal benefits.

CHAPTER 6

CRYSTAL PRACTICES FOR MOON SIGNS

The Moon, our lunar body, beams quietly as it is summoned each night into the dark skies. A primary aspect to your natal chart, this luminary is a deep reflection of how you feel inside. All the things that are typically kept hidden from the outside world exist here. This is part of your identity that needs to be experienced, felt, and acknowledged, though you don't display these traits to the outside world. Such is the nature of the subconscious mind: Its presence can only be seen through a smoke screen, yet it energetic imprints can be felt throughout your entire psyche.

Your Moon sign is all about working with the undercurrents of your individuality. Many of the practices in the upcoming chapter are meant to guide, nurture, and restore the pieces of you that react to emotional situations, as well as you to meet your own needs and boundaries. Through awareness and intention, these aspects of you will come into harmony and alignment. Get to know what makes you *feel* and open yourself up to the boundless gifts that await.

ARIES MOON: AURA CLEANSE

Aries Moon, you write your own rules and push yourself to new heights almost daily. You thrive on the freedom of the moment like a wildfire, and bravery courses through your veins, but this may occasionally cost you. Patience is a virtue, Aries Moon. To balance your reactivity, you'll be cooling off with an aura cleanse, meant to refresh you spiritually and bring you back to center.

✦ **Crystal: druzy quartz**

Druzy quartz works like selenite in that it removes uncomplimentary energies from your field, bringing peace and tranquility. This stone is ideal for "cooling" the system and providing a reset. After this exercise, you'll feel energetically cleansed from head to toe and more able to enjoy the sweet nectar of life.

1. Take your druzy crystal and say aloud, "I now cleanse my body, mind, and spirit. I invoke the crystalline energy within to wash away any uncomplimentary energies in my field and help me to be present in each moment. Guide my decisions to be deliberate and beneficial."

2. Complete a quick body scan. Note all of the places in your body that need attention. This may include recent or older physical injuries, tender spots.

3. Place the crystal on these areas for a minute or so, and then move on. At each area, ask for healing and just receive the crystal's energy.

4. Wave the crystal over your body a few times once your body scan is complete, swiping up from the root (pelvis) chakra to the crown (head).

5. Sit in quiet reflection, meditating with your druzy for as long as you like.

TAURUS MOON: EXALTED MOON CHARGE

Both solid ground and tenderness fill your soul, sweet Taurus Moon. You are a cosmic duality in motion and an open heart with strength and fortitude. You may face personal challenges when the need arises to flow like water, as your first response is always to hold on to that which you have determined is the best course of action. This practice is designed to help guide you through your stubborn moments and reveal to you the beauty of letting go.

✦ **Crystal: celestite**

Celestite is helpful for bringing clarity, peace, and understanding to any issue. In this exercise, you'll be working with the Moon's energy to release and let go of blockages. You'll be performing this ritual at night, so waiting for a full Moon for optimal charging is recommended, though you can charge your crystal at any point in the lunar cycle.

1. Take your celestite outside with you or to a windowsill that receives moonlight.

2. Pick an area of your life where you feel like energy is stuck.

3. Place your celestite down, and say aloud, "I call on angelic energies to help me now release _____. Help me to move on from _____ so I can be free to create new opportunities and blessings, which are on their way to me now. And so it is."

4. Allow your crystal to charge in the moonlight overnight.

5. Meditate with this crystal or keep in near you for the following Moon cycle, allowing it to clear your blockages.

6. Spend some mindful moments reflecting on the release of old energies.

7. Repeat the next Moon cycle with a new intention (or a past intention).

GEMINI MOON: FOUNDATIONAL FOCUS

You are a multifaceted being, Gemini Moon. Exploring each special moment, your flurried and curious mind beckons you into the wilderness of life. At times, you may use this as a distraction to avoid feeling your emotions. This practice will help you to build tolerance and focus so that you will be fully able to sit with your feelings.

✦ **Crystal: fluorite**

Fluorite, the stone of focus, offers clarity and is a container for your feelings. In this exercise, all you will need is your stone as you set your intentions and allow the crystal to do the heavy lifting. This is a simple practice of activating your space and doesn't take much time to perform. This works best if you are in a personal space, like your office or a bedroom.

1. Hold your fluorite in your palm and ask it to guide you to a space where you can set it down, to anchor the space.

2. Sit with your crystal quietly for a few moments. Ask yourself, "Is there anything that my heart needs to express right now?"

3. Allow time for your internal response to surface. Acknowledge whatever comes up for you and take a moment to do one thing in the moment that addresses your heart's feelings. Alternatively, you can write it down and make a plan to complete this step when the time is right.

4. Place your fluorite down in your chosen space wherever you feel the intention reminder would be best suited.

5. Leave it there for up to one week. Move to a new location and repeat as needed.

CANCER MOON: HEART OF THE OCEAN CLEANSE RITUAL

Cancer Moon, you are connected to your emotions at a cellular level. Each new Moon cycle brings new layers, and you are best honoring this in yourself when you respect both your light and your shadow sides. By working with the water element in a cleansing ritual, you'll learn to balance each cycle you are in.

✦ **Crystal: larimar**

✦ **Small bowl of water**

✦ **Hand towel**

In this exercise, you'll be harnessing the harmonizing quality of larimar and performing a short water ritual with intention. Larimar can help you access both past and future timelines, and aids in bringing in an extra dimension of purification and peace to your practice.

1. Fill a small bowl with cool water and set it beside your bed.

2. Begin a body scan with your larimar in hand. Notice where in your body you are storing trapped emotions.

3. Place your larimar directly on the parts of your body where you feel stuck emotions. This could be a tender area, an area of injury, or space where you feel heavy. If you aren't sure, place it on your heart or throat chakra.

4. Leave the crystal on that spot for up to three minutes, absorbing the energies as you breathe in peace, calm, and healing.

5. Rise your stone in the water when you feel finished, then dry it off.

6. Repeat steps three onward on all the places on your body which are calling for your attention. Allow the emotions to release and toss the water down the drain when you are finished.

LEO MOON: BREATHWORK RITUAL: TAKE FIVE

Leo Moon, you take on so much, for yourself and on behalf of your friends, coworkers, and family. Because of this, you have a natural need to de-stress. All the responsibilities of leadership can be a lot to manage. Learn to breathe your way to peace as you work with your breath to release unwanted energies and effortlessly calm your body and mind.

✦ **Crystal: sunstone**

Sunstone is a like a ray of sunshine bursting through the clouds. It can transmit light to anywhere in your body that needs it. Keep it in your palm or beside you as you work through a short breathwork ritual to eliminate tension. Breathwork is the practice of intentionally changing your breathing pattern in a conscious, intentional way.

1. Set a timer for five minutes. Breathe in deeply and slowly, taking a full inhalation as you count to seven and then release the breath without retaining it.

2. Notice the change from inhale to exhale as you release completely to a count of five.

3. Repeat this pattern for as long as you can. If your mind starts to wander, gently bring your attention back to the breath and keep going.

4. Play around with your breathing pattern after a few minutes. You might try decreasing the inhale/exhale count to five on the inhale and three on the outbreath.

5. After you have done this for five minutes, sit quietly with your sunstone, allowing it to energize and uplift you. Bask in your new clarity and expansion!

VIRGO MOON: SERENITY NOW

Virgo Moon, you are a rapturous lover of all things beautiful. You find a way to be neat and orderly in all areas of your life. However, this perfectionism can drain you of your vital energy, and your self-criticism can leave you feeling stressed. This exercise will help you to release tension and calm your nervous system when you have had a tough day. Letting go and surrendering a bit can bring in new blessings.

✦ **Crystal: lepidolite**

This practice is centered around the lepidolite crystal, which carries lithium energy. This energy gentle and soothing, calming and relaxing you. It helps you remove environmental electromagnetics from your space, soothing the nervous system. You may use one or two lepidolite plates or polished stones for this exercise.

1. Put on some meditation music or relaxing ambient sounds. Begin to breath mindfully, bringing your awareness to each breath.

2. Use your lepidolite plates or stones to absorb any negative energy. On each breath out, feel negative energy leaving your body and discharging into the stone(s).

3. Repeat for a few minutes, or until you are feeling light and peaceful. Say aloud, "I surrender to the natural peace and order of things. I am doing my best."

4. Place the lepidolite near a computer, Wi-Fi router, cell phone area, or television when it is not being used for practice. This will help to rid your environment of any sticky energies.

5. Enjoy weekly or monthly for optimal benefits.

LIBRA MOON:
CANDLELIGHT RITUAL

Being able to see and feel all sides of any situation makes you a remarkable mediator, Libra Moon. Though this doesn't burden you, you can occasionally become paralyzed with indecision within yourself when much is hanging in the balance. This practice helps the right choice make itself clear to you, while inviting in the energy of calming clarity.

+ **Crystal: agate**

+ **Several pieces of paper**

+ **Pen**

+ **2 tealight candles**

Agate crystal carries the energy of balance and new beginnings. This energy is nurturing, and opens you up to receive healing. This ritual is all about finding peace wherever you are and welcoming in new energies to help you on the next step in your path. If you are at a crossroads, this can help you to choose a direction.

1. Find a quiet place where you can sit with your thoughts undisturbed.

2. Write down on each piece of paper a choice you are weighing right now. Hold your agate as you take a few moments to do this.

3. Place each of your choices under a candle and light them both at the same time.

4. Say aloud, "I now ask for direction and clarity. Burn bright on the path of light! And so it is!"

5. Place your agate beside the candle altar. Use this time to meditate or sit quietly with your crystal, receiving its beneficial energy. Allow the candles to burn until they go out. The last one still burning is the choice you should go with.

SCORPIO MOON: SHADOW-WORK RITUAL

The light parts of ourselves are things we love and accept, while the shadow is a place that yearns for integration. Shadows include things we do not treasure about ourselves, such as anger, grief, projections, or shame. Scorpio Suns are full of mystery and intensity, but uncovering these things within yourself and bringing them into the light of love creates wholeness.

+ **Crystal: garnet**

+ **Some paper**

+ **Pen**

This practice uses garnet, a grounding stone for anchoring into your root and heart space, promoting feelings of safety and deep love. Garnet is extremely helpful when you are needing integration because it helps your heart to open and receive healing. For this exercise, find a place where you can think undisturbed for about 10 to 15 minutes.

1. Hold your garnet in your palm as you start to breathe deeply into your root chakra. Alternatively, you may place the garnet on your heart.

2. Say aloud, "I now invite my heart to open to a deeper love for myself."

3. Sit quietly for a bit. What have you been resisting inside yourself lately? Is there anything that you feel you dislike about yourself? Although these are limiting beliefs, bringing them to the surface through acknowledgment gives you a chance to heal.

4. Take a few moments to write down at least three things you'd like to change about yourself.

5. Place the paper under your garnet, and read the paper upon waking each day.

6. Say aloud, "I love myself for my ____. One way it has served me is ____." Do this for a week, or until you feel like you are starting to feel a shift.

SAGITTARIUS MOON: ALTAR OF TRANSFORMATION

You don't need a map to tell you where you are going; you are an adventurer who enjoys the fun of exploration and the change it brings, Sagittarius Moon. You are a philosopher and guide to your friends and family, but don't forget that you also need support with so much change is brewing. This practice will assist you in creating an intentional space to keep up with your ever-changing vision and journey.

✦ **Crystal: labradorite**

✦ **Candles, prayer or oracle cards, inspiring magazine clippings, special books, incense, figurines, flowers, etc.**

You'll be placing this stone in the center of your altar so that it radiates support to you when you are in need. Pick a quiet place in your bedroom, free from clutter, where you'll be assembling your altar.

1. Start by placing your labradorite in the center of the altar. State, "I dedicate this altar to self-improvement, and the version of myself I am becoming. And so it is!"

2. Arrange your items of choice on the altar around the labradorite. You may choose to create a crystal grid or simply lay your stones out in a pattern that feels good to you.

3. Build your altar throughout the month by adding or taking things away, but make sure only to leave up relevant images and items that will empower and inspire you daily.

4. Clear the altar at the end of the month and build a brand-new one, feeling free to reassign the labradorite crystal if its job supporting your transformation is complete.

CAPRICORN MOON: YOU ARE WORTHY HEART REWILDING RITUAL

Ruled by Saturn, the planet of discipline, your nature is structured and you live for praise, Capricorn Moon. Predictability is at the top of the list of your emotional needs, and you crave completion, organization, and wholeness. When things fall outside of this, you can become highly self-critical or cold to others.

✦ **Crystal: malachite**

✦ **Pen**

✦ **Paper**

Malachite is deeply loving, stabilizing, and grounding. For this exercise, you'll need a quiet space where you can lie down and rest for the meditation, plus about 10 minutes to write afterward. Use this exercise whenever you are having a rough day, are feeling out of alignment, or are disconnected from others.

1. Place your malachite on your heart chakra while lying down.

2. Spend some time thinking of all your accomplishments from this year, month, and week. Bring awareness to the happiness each one has brought into your life.

3. Let the malachite crystal expand your heart space with deep gratitude. Take a few moments to reflect on all the things you wish could have gone differently.

4. Tune back into your malachite crystal while lying down and, referring back to your list, repeat aloud, "I have the courage to accept that this is where I am right now. I forgive myself, as I am doing my best."

5. Let your crystal absorb any negative feelings that arise; breathe into it until you feel lighter, more open, and happier.

6. Repeat monthly for optimal benefits.

AQUARIUS MOON: FUTURE-SELF MEDITATION

Everything you create is inspired art, and your visions impact the world. In this exercise, we'll meditate with your future self to expand upon the visions of what you are creating and how that will be set up in reality.

+ **Crystal: turquoise**

+ **Pen**

+ **Journal**

This practice is centered around turquoise, a power–ful stone for third eye expansion and intuition. This stone is a protector against negative energies, and facil-itates wisdom and knowledge. Tur-quoise is perfect for helping you vision-quest new creations and ideas. Set aside about 20 minutes for this practice in a place where you'll be undisturbed.

1. Intend by saying aloud, "I now open my third eye. Allow me to receive what I need to know from my future self to create my highest timeline in this life."

2. Lie down facing up. Place your crystal on your third eye or in your palm.

3. Imagine yourself on a bench in a garden. Hang out there and just notice what you see. Eventually you notice a door. The door leads to a hallway. Open it.

4. At the end of the hall is another door, which you open. Your future self is inside.

5. Ask yourself anything you want to know.

6. Allow any information that is needed to be received. This includes any feelings, thoughts, visuals, colors, or words you are able to perceive.

7. When you feel complete, go back out the door and down the hallway. Come back to the garden and sit down. Open your eyes.

8. Write down anything you learned in the journal.

PISCES MOON: AKASHIC MEDITATION

Ruled by Neptune, the planet of dreams, your nature is fluid and ethereal, Pisces Moon. You often leave pieces of yourself behind in everything you do. This exercise will help you access the Akashic records, a spiritual space that contains the records of every moment of existence. Through these records, you can gain clarity and knowledge of your highest self.

✦ **Crystal: howlite**

✦ **Paper and journal**

The howlite crystal, a stone of remembering, awareness, and focus. This energy aids in opening the third eye and assists in recall during meditation. The Akashic records exist beyond your subconscious or conscious mind. Allow about 15 to 20 minutes for this exercise.

1. Begin by stating, "I ask my higher self to help me to access the akashic records. Please help me to heal and gain knowledge applicable to (myself, or another person). The records are now open."

2. Place your howlite on your third eye or crown space, or hold it in your palm.

3. Ask any questions you feel will benefit you to know. The answers you receive first are the correct ones. Responses from the akashic records are simple and straightforward. Trust the response(s) you receive.

4. Come back from your meditation once the information has stopped flowing to you and close the records by saying, "Thank you. The records are now closed."

5. Write down anything you learned. It helps to journal these things as soon as you can, for best memory recall.

6. Do this weekly for optimal benefits.

CHAPTER 7

CRYSTAL PRACTICES FOR RISING SIGNS

Your rising sign, or ascendant sign, is a bit more abstract to understand, as it has many nuances. While your Sun is the celestial body that illuminates your outward-projecting psyche, and the Moon is a reflection of your internal emotions, your rising sign determines how you are viewed by others. It is a filter through which your ego is expressed. This area of your chart covers what you expect from the world around you. Your persona is merely what you present for others to see, so it is one dimension or aspect of the sacred trinity (conscious, subconscious, and masks). Others will often connect you with this portion of your chart the most, because this is what they most often directly experience when interacting with you.

Your rising sign is all about working with the different parts of your outward persona, or your social personality. The practices in the upcoming chapter are meant to support your highest form of expression and overall approach to life. Through loving awareness and intention, you can direct others' impressions of you, as well as heal the part of you that is constantly witnessed.

ARIES RISING: INTENTIONAL TIGER

Aries Rising, you are driven by your physical vitality and the fire burning at the center of your soul. This makes you a natural leader who takes charge and always completes whatever you set out to accomplish. Occasionally, your personality can come across to others as larger-than-life or difficult to manage (you're usually the one managing things, anyway!). Slow down, and take things one step at a time to create an impression of powerful generosity

---

✦ **Crystal: tiger's eye**

Tiger's eye is a stone that enhances your solar plexus chakra and helps you feel grounded. This stone is ideal for balancing the system, as it can help you to gain knowledge and perspective to discern and decide. Whenever you wear it, allow the focus of your intention to surface naturally as you gaze at it throughout the day.

1. Take your tiger's eye crystal and say, "I choose to be present with my personal power. May this stone help me to slow down and be the intentional, powerful leader I was born to be."

2. Touch the tiger's eye to your solar plexus as you do this, allowing the energy to connect with your solar plexus chakra.

3. Place the crystal in a pocket, on your desktop, or in special place near you all day. Whenever you remember it, take it out and touch your solar plexus as a reminder of your intention.

4. Select a different intention that's relevant for you and repeat the practice with this or another stone in this book at any point of your choosing.

TAURUS RISING: HEART AFFIRMATIONS

You are caring, sensual, and lush, Taurus Rising. Your body, wardrobe, and lifestyle all reflect your concern about personal care. After all, these are needs that should be met first and foremost! People notice you, but you can come across as materialistic. Try balancing out your love of the material with a bit of affirmations to open your mind and spirit to higher realms.

✦ **Crystal: jade**

Jade is helpful for bringing peace, harmony, and joy to your friendships. It can help you to make wise choices for yourself. This practice will help you set aside material objects in lieu of more intentional practices. As a heart-opening crystal, jade will naturally lift your spirits and attract beauty and love to you, without you feeling as though you've sacrificed your self-care practices. Take some time in the morning to do this.

1. Hold your jade in your palm or place it on your heart.

2. Use these affirmations whenever you feel you need them. You may also choose to write them down on sticky notes or on a mirror you look into often.

Affirmations:

- My needs are met, and I feel the love that surrounds me.

- I am beautiful and strong.

- My heart opens to grace.

- I accept all that life offers me.

- I am aligned with peace and harmony.

- I am solely responsible for creating my own happiness.

- My happiness is a choice I get to make every day.

- I create abundance in and around me.

GEMINI RISING: REFLECTION: RELEASING LIMITING BELIEFS

Sweet and charming, you are known for your breezy wit and exceptional articulation when the situation calls for it, Gemini Rising. Other times, you can be very scattered. This flip-flop in the way you communicate may mean that others can't fully trust your stories, as they aren't sure what to expect when engaging in a conversation with you. This practice will help you to learn to trust yourself by releasing any limiting beliefs. With practice, your overall communication acumen will improve, helping you to shine as the intellectual you truly are.

+ **Crystal: blue sodalite**

+ **Paper and pen**

In this exercise, you'll be performing belief-work, a practice that helps eliminate internal negativities holding you back. Limiting beliefs are thoughts that inhibit your creation mode, and include negative self-talk,or the little voice inside that wants to stop you out of fear.

1. Take out your blue sodalite and hold it in your hand for a few moments. Then state, "I now focus my intention on purging any limiting beliefs held within me. I open myself to the expression of my highest truth. I am clear, confident, and articulate."

2. Make a short list of limiting thoughts that come to mind when you feel ready.

3. Fold the page in half once finished with your list, and make an "opposite" list. What would the list say if it were to be a *limitless* list?

4. Place your blue sodalite on your throat space or hold it while reading aloud from your limitless list. Feel each statement resonate within your body and mind.

CANCER RISING:
REPARENTING RITUAL

You are maternal and caring at your core, Cancer Rising. This quality is apparent to anyone who meets you. The downside is that your empathy can make you seem moody and temperamental. This practice will help you heal your unprocessed emotions by honing your reparenting skills. You are your own greatest mother, teacher, helper, and guide.

✦ **Crystal: peach moonstone**

Peach moonstone is known for its ability to harmonize and connect you to the Divine Mother energy within yourself. This stone is meant to bring out your soft side while encouraging you to form healthy boundaries, helping you become the expert listener and responsible friend you always have been inside your shell.

1. Place the peach moonstone on your heart. Say aloud, "I ask for grace to help me in finding the places inside that need attention and healing. Allow me to explore the depths with loving awareness to uncover any hidden emotions or beliefs holding me back. And so it is."

2. Take several breaths into your heart space. Ask yourself: What do I need help with emotionally right now? Is there anything I did not receive when I was younger that could be affecting my emotional state right now? Is there anything I can give myself in this or a future moment that will help me to feel my best?

3. Spend some time with these questions. Take time to listen to yourself. Write it down if necessary.

4. Spend a few minutes at the end of your practice allowing the peach moonstone to soothe and heal your heart until you feel lighter and complete with the exercise.

LEO RISING: HEART OF GOLD OPEN-HEART MEDITATION

A leader with a heart of gold is who you really are inside, Leo Rising. You naturally dazzle, but people who are not close to you may see you as attention-seeking and self-concerned. This practice will allow your true essence to shine through, without the needing to perform for anyone else.

✦ **Crystal: amazonite**

Amazonite is an incredible heart healer, helping you to exude love and acceptance, and to know peace, even if you are not the center of attention. Engendering childlike wonder, amazonite calls you back to your innocence, and recalibrates your nervous system so you can feel stabilized and harmonious sharing love and attention with those around you.

1. Place your amazonite on your heart. Breathe in deeply and slowly, taking full inhalations and exhalations.

2. State, "I now release any attachment to the part of me that needs to be seen at all times. I have all the love I need inside me. I open myself to the wonders of acceptance and sharing. And so it is."

3. Bring a warm smile to your face, like you have just seen an old friend. Feel the quality of the warmth radiating from you.

4. Let the stone melt anything in your heart that feels unaligned. Do this for 5 to 10 minutes, or until you feel lighter.

5. Carry your amazonite around with you as a reminder of your intention to share from a space of honesty and true connection.

VIRGO RISING: GOOD MORNING WAKING MEDITATION

You show up in the world as comported, resourced, and capable, Virgo Rising. Your precise and deliberate manner is award-worthy, but you can sometimes get lost in your own perfectionism. Be careful not to cast your expectations on others. This practice will help you to reset and realign your intentions before your day gets started so you can avoid projecting your perfectionism onto others to avoid disappointment.

✦ **Crystal: apophyllite**

This practice is centered around the apophyllite crystal, which carries angelic, uplifting energy. Having it close to you as you start your day will help you to align with these energies within yourself, and balance any expectations you are holding for yourself and anyone else.

1. Grab your apophyllite immediately upon waking or place it near your crown or on your pillow by your head.

2. Stay in bed and do not check emails or look at your phone. Do nothing to engage with the outside world. Simply be in an awake and aware state.

3. Begin to breathe mindfully, bringing your awareness to each inhale and exhale.

4. Relish in your divinity and the beauty around you. Spend these moments in gratitude for everything you have created and everything you will create.

5. Release any thoughts that are holding you back with loving awareness. Just be here now without needing to change anything.

6. Allow any message from your angels and guides to come to you in their own time.

LIBRA RISING: PURIFY YOUR LIFE RITUAL

You are easy to like and get along with, Libra Rising. Your elegance is charming, and you are rarely caught up in disagreements with others. You can, however, let how others view you rule your life. This practice will help you to clear your personal spaces of any negative projections cast upon you by yourself or by others.

✦ Crystal: selenite

Selenite carries the energy of tranquility and mental clarity. This energy is cleansing and will help give you an energetic reset. Selenite is a master cleansing stone, so use it often in daily practice. There are so many ways to use it, so get creative with how you incorporate this crystal into your life. (Pro tip: Sprinkle selenite shavings into paint and repaint your doorways with it if you feel called to do so.)

1. Declutter your living environment. Toss anything that isn't bringing you excitement or reminds you of outdated versions of yourself.

2. Take your selenite and wand it over the doorways and by the corners of the room(s) you use most often. Say, "I now cleanse this space and welcome in new energies that align with my highest vibrational state. And so it is."

3. Wave your crystal over your body and feel the negative energies lifting.

4. Use it as a plate for your jewelry and other crystals. By doing this, you'll be giving them a nice reset, as well.

5. Welcome in feelings of lightness and clarity as you bask in your new energetic space.

SCORPIO RISING: REBIRTH RITUAL

Ruled by deep-seeking and transformative Pluto, your essence is truly that of the shape-shifter, Scorpio Rising. The way in which you show up for yourself by consistently offering yourself deeper understanding and acceptance is what polishes this stone into a diamond. You are constantly shedding your skin, and you have no qualms about sinking into the darkness to reemerge powerfully and skillfully. This practice will help you cross the threshold of your transformation phases.

✦ **Crystal: obsidian**

✦ **Some soil**

Obsidian is one of the most powerful grounding stones and assists you in crossing the threshold between life and death. Sometimes when part of us evolves, there can be a mourning period for the old version of yourself. Obsidian is helpful in carrying you through this in-between stage and supporting the new version of you.

1. Pull your obsidian out and bury it in some soil when you feel yourself in the middle of a personal transformation. If this is outside, feel free to mark the spot with another stone on top.

2. Say aloud, "I bury the past, as a new me emerges. I call in support in all its forms to get me through these waves of the unknown. I go fearlessly into the darkness by letting go and fully allowing this transformation process. And so it is."

3. Leave the stone there overnight, or for as long as needed. During this time, you will feel yourself moving through change. Remember that seeds are buried before they break through the soil into the light.

4. Unearth your obsidian when you feel the transformation is well underway. Sleep with it under your pillow to tap into your new patterning with strength and stability.

SAGITTARIUS RISING: CAT-COW BALANCING RITUAL

Adventurous and courageous are hallmarks of your fire sign, Sagittarius rising. You exude confidence and are loaded with the charm and personality to get others to believe in themselves, too. This practice will help you with your embodiment of grace, through an aligned yoga posture called cat-cow. Cat-cow helps bring balance to your nervous system by balancing your brain waves and awakening your spine, allowing excess energy to move through you effortlessly.

+ **Crystal: red jasper**
+ **Mat**

Red jasper is super helpful in grounding your physical body. This crystal can help you bring out your inner strength. As a fire sign, it's important to connect your mind and body physically through embodiment practices. Do as many reps as you can in a minute and take a break if you need to, or if you feel any pinching.

1. Place your red jasper beside you, and make sure you can see it as you move through this posture.

2. Begin in the tabletop position on a yoga mat. Your hands and knees will be on the floor, your spine should be neutral, and your head and neck focused straight ahead.

3. Come into cat pose. Inhale as you round your back upward, curling your head down and tucking your hips forward.

4. Exhale as you begin to change positions to cow pose. Arch your back down as your head lifts up toward the ceiling, eyes to the sky. Keep your shoulders pulled back, away from your ears.

5. Hold the cat-cow pose for a minute, or until you feel your energy shift to a calm and peaceful state.

CAPRICORN RISING: CRYSTAL-GRID RITUAL

You are a superior protector and parental ally for your close group of friends. People think of you as reliable and steady, both physically and mentally. In general, your challenge is to work on your vulnerability and not come off to others as defensive or condescending. Soften up your facade by building a daily intention practice with a crystal grid, amplifying your self-care!

+ **Crystal: clear quartz**

+ **Other crystals you would like to incorporate into a grid**

The clear quartz amplifies, purifies, and enhances the energies of other stones and the environment in which it's placed. Clear quartz inspires wisdom and helps you clarify your truths. It can be used along with other crystals to intensify their effects. You'll be using clear quartz in a crystal grid.

1. Select the crystals you would like to place in your grid according to their metaphysical properties. Your selection should include at least one clear quartz crystal and one "master crystal."

2. Place the generator at the center of the grid. The generator is a single-terminated crystal pointing up toward the sky helping to focus energy.

3. Build a mandala-like lattice around your generator. You can make this as intricate or complex as you like or keep it simple. Supplement your stones with natural treasures like pebbles, shells, or garden stones if you don't have enough crystals to complete your vision.

4. Pick up your master stone, which will sit outside the grid to amplify it, and say, "I open myself to amplifying the good in my life. I surrender to life's flow and allow others to see the real me. And so it is." You may also add other intentions.

AQUARIUS RISING: INSPIRED WRITING WITH YOUR HIGHER SELF

Aquarius Rising, you are pure, unconditional love, always ensuring the underdog feels like they belong. A champion for humanity and the arts with your innovative take on things, you often inspire others. However, you can sometimes show up as impartial, unfeeling, and a bit robotic. Cultivate sensitivity toward others by connecting with your higher self and building a strong sense of vulnerability within yourself.

✦ **Crystal: aquamarine**

✦ **Journal and pen**

This stone helps you to quiet your mind and reduce stress, providing support when you feel overwhelmed. It's angelic-feel assists in connecting you to higher channels of communication with your guides and Higher Self. In this practice, you will connect to your Higher Self through a process called automatic writing, or freewriting.

1. Place your aquamarine beside you. You may meditate with it before you begin.

2. Make a list of questions that you have about yourself. These should be focused on self-improvement, with a goal of betterment through self-inquiry.

3. Say aloud, "I now connect to my higher self. May all that is needed be known."

4. Gaze at your crystal as you sit until your pen begins to move in response. Let go of control. Write down any information that is received during your transmission.

5. Do not try to understand or read the writing in the moment. Just allow the answers to flow through you onto the page. When the information has stopped flowing, the session is complete.

6. Do this weekly or as often as needed for optimal benefits.

PISCES RISING:
ENERGY-CLEARING RITUAL

Pisces Rising, you have such fluid and adaptable approach to life that you truly are the ocean. Your shores are peaceful and calm, and your sensitivity is a bastion of softness. However, in your lowest moments, you have a tendency toward escapism and victimhood, and you may feel lost. An important part of your daily ritual should include managing your energy, as well as any baggage that others (consciously or unconsciously) leave at your doorstep. This practice will help you to create a ritual daily reset so you can ground yourself in your own tranquility.

✦ **Crystal: black kyanite**

Black kyanite is extremely powerful, connecting you with your center for grounding and stability. Kyanite (both blue and black) are excellent stones to enhance communication, allowing your truth to surface naturally. This crystal is also a prime choice for cleansing rituals and a favorite among energy healers for its clearing and protection capabilities.

1. Say aloud, "I now clear away all energies that are not serving my highest benefit. I remove any energy that isn't mine and doesn't belong to me, and anything uncomplimentary to my highest path. And so it is."

2. Use your black kyanite as a "fan" (the natural shape is fanlike, so this one is easy to imagine) to make several swipes up and down your torso, arms, legs, and all parts that you are inspired to cleanse. Wand the energy away from your body. You may even visualize it as black smoke blowing away and dissolving.

3. Place your kyanite on your root chakra. Say aloud, "I now ground my own energy into my body. My body is a vessel of light and energy, and I am safe to experience it in its sovereignty and fullness. And so it is."

CHAPTER 8

Q & A

Now that you have some solid suggestions to get you going on your path, you will be able to start understanding the relationships between the signs, elements, modalities, and planets, not to mention the properties and energies of many widely used crystals. There are many pairings that you can begin to make for yourself now that you have experimented with your own sign trilogy. If you wish to truly harness all that astrology and crystals have to offer, continue practicing and document your journey. Over time, the information in this book will become second nature and your confidence will increase as you grow spiritually.

The following chapter helps answer some common questions that pop up when you are just starting out on your journey through astrology and crystals. It is my hope that you'll be able to learn the intricacies of your own big three before moving onto more advanced chart details, which are not covered in this book. Astrology and crystals represent a lifetime of practice and study, so keep growing.

Q I've heard Mercury retrograde can be chaotic and things often go sideways. Which crystal should I reach for during this time?

A Mercury retrograde is a period when the planet Mercury appears to move backward or "retreat" in the sky. During this time, it is a common superstition that communication and relationships are affected negatively. The short answer is that if you have a positive Mercury placement in your chart, you'll be relatively unaffected. If you do not, you may see exes return or electronic interference. If you notice that you experience these negative effects during a period of retrograde, you can use blue kyanite, blue sodalite, or lapis lazuli to facilitate communication and smooth your crunchy Mercurial ride.

Q Can I substitute one crystal for another and still reap the rewards for my sign?

A You can swap the crystals in the practices if you feel called to work with another stone. I encourage you to read about the different properties that each stone offers and select a complimentary stone for the corresponding exercise. In general, signs are categorized by their element, and each element matches a chakra. Because each chakra has a specific color or energy frequency, you can easily start to translate each sign into stones according to their vibration. For example, Aries is a fire sign, and the fire element is associated with the root chakra and the solar plexus chakra. A red, orange, or yellow stone like calcite or red jasper would be complimentary to a fire sign.

Q Is it possible to do the crystal practices for other people if I know their Sun/Moon/rising signs?

A Anything is possible. However, the practices work best when they are experienced directly. Your intention is personal for you, and the belief work and time spent on a ritual help to reinforce your specific intention. It is better to complete exercises on behalf of others if they are simple and designed as such. Examples of this could be space-clearing with selenite, building a crystal grid, or dedicating an altar or vision board to someone to help them in their healing journey.

Q If I am not sure of my Moon or rising signs, can I still participate in the practices?

A As discussed early in the book, you will be unable to distill exact Moon or rising signs without a specific time and place of birth. If you are unsure of this information, you can still work with your Sun sign.

Q Is there any wrong way to use a crystal?

A Crystals work alongside your intention to help you. There is no wrong way to use a crystal. However, there are guides for proper treatment and care that suggest ways to handle different crystals. For example, some crystals with a low Mohs (hardness) rating should not get wet, and others scratch easily, so you shouldn't charge them with other stones.

Q Is there any benefit/drawback to using the practices along with lunar cycles?

A Some people prefer to wait for a new or full Moon, or other part of the lunar cycle, to perform the exercises or rituals in this book. While it can be very powerful to align this work with the Moon's cycle, it isn't necessary. Many spiritual guides promote beginning new rituals or practices on the new Moon, to invite in new blessings. If you follow this path, then aim to complete the ritual for that specific intention by the full Moon, which is the time of completion or harvest.

Q If my natal chart is like the blueprint for my life, how much of life is fate versus free will?

A We always have a choice in how we show up in the world. Although there are several ways that your "coding" can unfurl in your lifetime, you also have the choice to evolve yourself past your own limitations. Signs, planets, and transits will show you what you are working with, but they won't show you what you are going to choose to do with that. There are so many ways your chart can work for you, so don't get caught up in believing in any one destiny. Life is about the journey and not the destination, and the journey is what you make it.

Q What if I don't live near a crystal shop—can I purchase crystals online?

A There are a few resources mentioned at the end of this book, which you can use to purchase crystals online. Though connecting with crystals in person is best, there is nothing wrong with connecting with a crystal virtually first. It is more important to find a reputable source for crystals, whether virtual or in person, with ethical business practices. Supporting small mines or individuals rather than large shops brings more profits directly to the miners who work hard to procure your crystals. Unfortunately, that is not always possible to determine when buying stones. The best way to determine this when no one knows is to sit quietly with the crystals' energy and ask.

Q Is the Vedic system of astrology compatible with these practices?

A Vedic or Hindu astrology, contains rich culture, as well as ancient astrology dating back to 10,000 BCE. Similar to modern Western astrology, it serves as a road map to help us understand our human experience. However, Vedic astrology uses the sidereal calendar for zodiac calculations, and Western astrology uses the tropical calendar. Because the calendars are different, the signs run to different parts of the month, and you may show up under a separate sign under the Vedic context. The information in this book is based on Western astrology, though if you know your Vedic chart, you may adapt the practices and use them accordingly.

A FINAL WORD

Congratulations for making it through the early stages of your astrology and crystals journey. You now have the tools to begin exploring astrology and crystals, and interpret your findings to assist in your own expansion. Astrology is rich in symbolism, and it can easily become an entire life's work, as there is so much to know. Be patient with yourself while you are learning and building your skills. It's perfectly acceptable to start with the basics and stay there until you are ready to move on to reading finer aspects of a natal chart (like current transits, conjunctions, and planetary placements).

Crystals have a lot to share with you as well. They take time to get to know personally and develop a relationship with. Remember that they each possess their own consciousness and you will naturally desire to work with some stones over others. Trust your intuition and let it be your guide. You can use your newfound wisdom to improve your relationships and lifestyle if you set aside some time to listen and learn from your crystals. Bless your journey ahead, and may the Sun illuminate your path, always!

GLOSSARY

ascendant sign: This is another term for your rising sign. This point of your birth chart shows the sign that was in the sky on the eastern horizon at the time of your birth. This represents an integration of all aspects of your chart, and some systems believe it to be the most important part of your personal astrology.

aspect: When two or more planets line up in the sky at certain angles, this is known as ""aspecting" each other. The energies may mix and mingle, creating various harmonies or disharmonic effects.

big three: Your Sun, Moon, and rising (ascendant) sign make up your big three in astrology. These primary astrology signs rule over certain areas of your life. For example, the Sun is your outward personality, the Moon is your inner personality, and your rising sign is the mask you wear around others.

birth chart: An astrological chart representing the positions of planets in the zodiac at the time of your birth. This is also known as a natal chart, and knowing the time, place, and location of your birth is necessary to obtain your exact zodiac placements.

crystal grid: A formation of separate crystals that creates a system amplifying the entire group of crystals. Often there is a charger at the center of the crystal grid and several clear quartz crystals holding a special intention, while supplemental crystals fill in the rest of the grid, giving it special characteristics.

crystal system: Systems used to group crystals by their symmetry. There are six crystal systems: monoclinic, triclinic, triagonal, cubic, orthorhombic, and tetragonal.

element: The four elements—water, earth, fire, and air—govern three signs apiece and play a role in the classification and predictability of each sign.

inclusion: A material trapped inside a mineral at the time of its formation.

lattice: The ordered arrangement of atoms, ions, or molecules inside a crystal.

mineral: A mineral is a naturally occurring solid with a specific chemical composition.

Mohs hardness scale: A measure of a mineral's hardness and resistance to scratching. This scale is from 1 to 10, with 10 being the hardest substance (diamond).

transit: When a planet moves in the sky, this is called a transit. It may be moving into a new zodiac house or sign, or going retrograde.

RESOURCES

BOOKS

Askinosie, Heather, and Timmi Jandro. *Crystal Muse: Everyday Rituals to Tune into the Real You*. San Diego: Hay House, 2018. Rituals and crystal practices to enhance your understanding and abilities in working with crystal energy from two old-school crystal experts!

Bonewitz, Ronald. *Rock and Gem: The Definitive Guide to Rocks, Minerals, Gemstones, and Fossils*. London: DK Publishing, 2008. Everything you ever want to know about crystals, from a scientific lens.

Edington, Louise. *The Complete Guide to Astrology: Understanding Yourself, Your Signs, and Your Birth Chart*. Emeryville, California: Rockridge Press, 2020. In-depth definitions and beyond-the-basics for people looking to deepen their relationship with the planets and astrology.

Edut, Ophira, and Tali Edut. *The AstroTwins' 2022 Horoscope: The Complete Yearly Astrology Guide for Every Zodiac Sign*. New York: Astrostyle, 2021. Accurate horoscopes for the year ahead, updated annually!

Hall, Judy. *The Crystal Bible*. Lola, WI: Krause Publications, 2003. Crystals from A to Z and their metaphysical healing properties.

Freed, Jennifer. *Use Your Planets Wisely: Master Your Ultimate Potential with Psychological Astrology*. Boulder, CO: Sounds True Publishing, 2020. A practical guide to evolving through your personal astrology.

Goldschneider, Gary. *The Astrology of You and Me: How to Understand and Improve Every Relationship in Your Life*. Philadelphia: Quirk Books, 2018. Snarky and entertaining, Gary weighs-in on how to manage every relationship in your life, depending on your (and their) personal astrology.

Wright, Katie-Jane. *Crystals: How to Tap into Your Infinite Potential through the Healing Power of Crystals*. New Jersey: Aster, 2019. Intuitive Katie-Jane's years of experience channeling crystal energy. A book on selecting and caring for your crystal companions.

ETHICALLY SOURCED CRYSTAL SHOPS

AndCrystals.com, @andcrystals

LemuriaCrystalShop.com, @lemuriacrystalshop

SoulConnectionStore.com

WildlingHeart.com, @wildling_heart

PODCASTS

That's So Retrograde: Wellness and Beyond with Stephanie Simbari and Elizabeth Kott. Podcast on thought leaders in health, beauty, astrology, empowering listeners to find the guru within.

The Rising Sign with Colin Bedell. Popular and loved, Colin gives his entertaining outlooks on all things astrology and explains how celestial events impact our daily lives in a practical, no-nonsense way.

WEBSITE

Magic of I
MagicOfI.com

REFERENCES

AstroTwins. "The 12 Houses of the Horoscope Wheel." Astrostyle. April 25, 2021. astrostyle.com/learn-astrology /the-12-zodiac-houses/.

Beaudoin, Heather. "Crystals vs. Gemstones—What Are the Differences?", January 28, 2021. tinybandit.com/blog /crystals-vs-gemstones.

Grant, Eva Taylor. "The 2 Zodiac Signs You Connect with Most Deeply, Based on Your Sign." Bustle. Bustle, January 16, 2019. bustle.com/p/the-2-zodiac-signs-you-connect-with -most-deeply-based-on-your-sign-15829512.

Harlow, George E., and Joseph Peters. *Minerals and Gems: From the American Museum of Natural History*. New York: Abbeville, 2003.

Haxworth, Caryl. "Crystal Healing Properties." Charmsoflight .com. 2010–2021. charmsoflight.com

Kahn, Nina. "The Modalities in Astrology Say so Much about Your Personality." *Bustle*. August 16, 2021. bustle.com /life/is-your-zodiac-sign-cardinal-fixed-mutable-heres-what -it-all-means-19418010.

Keen Editorial Staff. "3 Different Types of Astrology You Should Know." Keen. August 16, 2020. keen.com/articles /astrology/3-different-types-of-astrology-you-should-know.

Magliochetti, Michaela. "Zodiac Planets, Explained: Here's What Each Celestial Body Says about You." PureWow. November 9, 2020. purewow.com/wellness/zodiac-planets.

Rickard, David T. Pyrite: *A Natural History of 'Fool's Gold*. New York: Oxford University Press, 2020.

INDEX

A

Abundance All Day, 91
Agate, 67
Air signs, 12
Akashic Meditation, 111
Altar of Transformation, 108
Altars, 31
Amazonite, 62
Amethyst, 78
Apophyllite, 65
Aquamarine, 80
Aquarius
  about, 10, 44–45
  as eleventh house, 19
  Future-Self Meditation, 110
  Inspired Writing with Your
    Higher Self, 123
  Vision-Quest Ritual, 97
Aries
  about, 8, 37
  Aura Cleanse, 100
  as first house, 18
  Intentional Tiger, 113
  Mirror Dancing, 87
Ascendants. See Rising signs
Astrology
  about, 3, 20
  benefits of, 4–6
  crystals and, 19–20, 32, 35
  origins of, 3–4
  as a practice, 19
Astronomy, 3
Aura Cleanse, 100

B

Balancing Moonstone
  Meditation, 93
Birth charts, 6. See also
  Natal charts
Black kyanite, 83
Blue sodalite, 56
Breathwork Ritual: Take Five, 104

C

Cancer
  about, 8–9, 39–40
  as fourth house, 18
  Heart of the Ocean
    Cleanse Ritual, 103
  Home Sweet Home, 90
  Reparenting Ritual, 116
Candelight Ritual, 106
Capricorn
  about, 10, 44
  Crystal-Grid Ritual, 122
  Earth Walk & Charge, 96
  as tenth house, 19
  You Are Worthy Heart
    Rewilding Ritual, 109
Cardinal signs, 13
Carnelian, 48
Cat-Cow Balancing Ritual, 121
Celestite, 52
Chakras, 29–30
Chinese astrology, 3
Chrysocolla, 57
Citrine, 60
Clear quartz, 77

Crystal-Grid Ritual, 122
Crystal grids, 29, 31
Crystallization, 23
Crystals. *See also specific*
   about, 22, 33
   astrology and, 19–20, 32, 35
   benefits of, 25–26
   caring for, 27, 28–29, 127
   and chakras, 29–30
   charging, 29
   choosing, 27
   cleansing, 27, 28
   healing power of, 32
   history of, 22
   misconceptions about, 26–27
   natural vs. manufactured, 23
   origins of, 23
   practicing for others, 126–127
   sourcing, 24, 128
   substituting, 126
   using, 28

D

Dreamwork Ritual, 98
Druzy quartz, 49

E

Earth signs, 11–12
Earth Walk & Charge, 96
Elements, 11–12
Energy, refocusing, 25
Energy-Clearing Ritual, 124
Exalted Moon Charge, 101

F

Fate, vs. free will, 128
Fire signs, 11
Fixed signs, 13
Fluorite, 55
Foundational Focus, 102
Four Corners Walking
   Meditation, 88
Full moon, 14
Future-Self Meditation, 110

G

Garnet, 69
Gemini
   about, 8, 38–39
   Foundational Focus, 102
   Highest-Self Meditation, 89
   Reflection: Releasing
      Limiting Beliefs, 115
   as third house, 18
Good Morning Waking
   Meditation, 118

H

Healing, 25, 32
Heart Affirmations, 114
Heart of Gold Open-Heart
   Meditation, 117
Heart of the Ocean
   Cleanse Ritual, 103
Highest-Self Meditation, 89
Home Sweet Home, 90
Houses, 17–19
Howlite, 82

I

Inspired Writing with Your
   Higher Self, 123
Intentional Tiger, 113
Intentions, 22, 26

J

Jade, 53
Jasper, red, 74
Jupiter, 16

K

Kundalini Awakening, 94
Kyanite, black, 83

L

Labradorite, 70
Lapis lazuli, 81
Larimar, 58
Lattices, 22, 23
Lemurian quartz, 54
Leo
   about, 9, 40
   Abundance All Day, 91
   Breathwork Ritual:
      Take Five, 104
   as fifth house, 18
   Heart of Gold Open-Heart
      Meditation, 117
Lepidolite, 64
Libra
   about, 9, 41–42
   Balancing Moonstone
      Meditation, 93

   Candelight Ritual, 106
   Purify Your Life
      Ritual, 119
   as seventh house, 18
Lunar cycles, 14, 127

M

Malachite, 76
Mars, 16
Mercury, 16
Mercury retrograde, 126
Mirror Dancing, 87
Modalities, 12–13
Mohs hardness
      scale, 28–29
Moon
   about, 15
   phases, 14, 127
   signs, 6, 7, 99, 127. *See
      also specific*
Moonstone
   peach, 59
   rainbow, 66
Mutable signs, 13

N

Natal charts, 3, 5, 128
Negative feelings and
      emotions, 26
Neptune, 17
New moon, 14

O

Obsidian, 71

P

Peach moonstone, 59
Pisces, 45–46
  about, 10
  Akashic Meditation, 111
  Dreamwork Ritual, 98
  Energy-Clearing
      Ritual, 124
  as twelfth house, 19
Planets, 15–17
Pluto, 17
Purify Your Life Ritual, 119
Pyrite, 72

Q

Quartz
  clear, 77
  druzy, 49
  lemurian, 54
  rose, 63
  smoky, 51

R

Rainbow moonstone, 66
Rebirth Ritual, 120
Red jasper, 74
Reflection: Releasing
      Limiting Beliefs, 115
Relationship compatibility,
      5–6, 7–8
Reparenting Ritual, 116
Rising signs, 6, 7, 112, 127.
      See also specific
Rose quartz, 63

S

Sagittarius
  about, 10, 43
  Altar of Transformation, 108
  Cat-Cow Balancing
      Ritual, 121
  as ninth house, 18
  Solar-Charged Abundance, 95
Saturn, 16
Scorpio
  about, 9, 42–43
  as eighth house, 18
  Kundalini Awakening, 94
  Rebirth Ritual, 120
  Shadow-Work Ritual, 107
Selenite, 68
Serenity Now, 105
Serpentine, 73
Shadow-Work Ritual, 107
Smoky quartz, 51
Sodalite, blue, 56
Solar-Charged Abundance, 95
Sun
  about, 15
  Abundance All Day, 91
  Highest-Self Meditation, 89
  signs, 6, 86. See also specific
  transits, 36
Sunstone, 61

T

Taurus
  about, 8, 37–38
  Exalted Moon Charge, 101

Four Corners Walking
   Meditation, 88
   Heart Affirmations, 114
   as second house, 18
Tiger's eye, 50
Tourmaline, 75
Transits, 4–5, 36
Tropical astrology, 3
Tropic of Cancer, 3
Tropic of Capricorn, 3
Turquoise, 79

U

Uranus, 17

V

Vedic astrology, 4, 128–129
Venus, 16
Virgo
   about, 9, 41
   Good Morning Waking
      Meditation, 118

Serenity Now, 105
   as sixth house, 18
   Water Cleansing Ritual, 92
Vision-Quest Ritual, 97

W

Waning moon, 14
Water Cleansing Ritual, 92
Water signs, 12
Waxing moon, 14
Western astrology, 3

Y

You Are Worthy Heart
   Rewilding Ritual, 109

Z

Zodiac
   houses, 17–19
   signs, 7–10. *See also*
      specific

ACKNOWLEDGMENTS

I'd like to thank my beloved partner, Will, for supporting and encouraging me to give the gift of voice to this work and birth it into the world.

Thank you to my friends and family for your understanding, love, and support.

Deep gratitude for my meditation and Reiki students who inspire me daily, proving that reality is illustrious and multidimensional.

Thank you to Skyla the Frenchie, who is always my loving sidekick and watched this book come into creation, word by word.

ABOUT THE AUTHOR

 APRIL PFENDER is the founder of Golden Light Alchemy, a healing-focused collective that combines her years of trauma-informed healing with Reiki and other various healing modalities. April is a Reiki master teacher, quantum and sound healer, and meditation instructor who has been studying, teaching, and writing about self-empowerment for years. You can find her other books *Chakra Balance*, *Essential Chakra Meditation,* and *The Complete Guide to Chakras* out now. Her work has carried her through a deeply spiritual journey of healing, and her focus is now primarily helping people through their own healing and ascension journeys.

April is a daughter, a mother, a lover, a healer, a guide, and a teacher to many. She currently resides on the East Coast with her beloved partner and hosts virtual and in-person training classes, as well as retreats.

CPSIA information can be obtained
at www.ICGtesting.com
Printed in the USA
JSHW030325040522
25500JS00003B/6

9 781638 784395